AF290664

Leaves of Autumn

International Poetry

Edited by

Gino Leineweber

Verlag Expeditionen

Publisher: Verlag Expeditionen, 2018
Leaves of Autumn
International Poems
Edited by Gino Leineweber

Cover: Leelanau County, Mi, USA 2013
Photo: Gino Leineweber
Design: Birgitta Sjöblom

ISBN 978-3-943863-76-5

Autumn is a second spring
when every leaf's a flower.
Albert Camus

Table of Contents

Table of Contents

SOLGUN YÜZÜ HAYATIN

Ahmet Özer, Türkiye

güzdür / yeryüzü solgun ışıklarla gelir
geceler ayrılık taşır yanında
babanın gidişi anımsanır uzaklara
yataklar biraz daha soğur yıldızlar üşür.

güzdür / pencerenin ardından gözlenir hayat
kuşlar sürü sürü yolcudur göklerde
sular çekilir derinlere uykudadır toprak
şiirden romana yolculuktur düşlerin derinliği.

güzdür / yıldırımlar düşer ovalara
çoban çocuklardır yitiveren sürülerin ardında
insan kabuğuna çekilir anılara yaslanarak
hüzzam şarkılar demlenir iklimler değişirken.

güzdür / doğayı uykuya götüren zaman
binlerce çiçeği eker düşlerimize
bahara sefer eyleyen gökyüzüdür isyanımıza tanık
mevsimlerin çınladığı fotoğraftır önümüzde.

PALE FACE OF LİFE

Ahmet Özer, Turkey
Translated by Hilal Karahan, Turkey

it is the autumn / the earth comes with pale lights
the nights carry separation with them
father's going is recalled far away
the beds get colder, the stars feel chilly.

it is the autumn / life is observed behind the window
they travel into the sky, a bevy of birds
the water is withdrawn to deeps, the earth sleeps
it is a journey from poetry to novel, the depth of
    dreams.

it is the autumn / it bombards the plains with
    thunderbolts
they are the shepherd boys disappearing behind the
    droves
man leaning to memories withdraws into solitude
huzzam[1] songs brew while the climates change.

it is the autumn / time, leading nature to sleep,
plants thousands of flowers into our dreams
the sky is the witness to our rebellion in this
    expedition to the spring
in front of us, there is a photo in which seasons are
    ringing

---

1 Huzzam Makamı (from the Arabic word مقام) is a system
of melody types used in Arabic, Persian and Turkish classical music.
It provides a complex set of rules for composing and performance.

HALLOWEEN

Alexandru Cetăţeanu, Romania/Canada

Spre noiembrie - întâi,
Lume multă, agitată.
Într-un val de bucurie
E Canada prinsă toată.

Vălmăşaguri de culori
Zi de zi şi sărbătoare;
Halloween-u-i nebunie
Pentru mic şi pentru mare.

Peste tot, Dracula-n frunte.
Măşti din lumea cu strigoi,
Cu stafii şi cu vedenii
Ce-şi arată dinţii goi.

Zarvă, zarvă şi iar zarvă
Cete de copii, coloane:
Bat la uşi şi bat la porţi
Primesc fructe şi bomboane.

... Simt colindul de la noi
Pe sub marile căciuli.
Lumea asta este plină
De poveşti... cimilituri...

HALLOWEEN
Alexandru Cetăţeanu, (Romania, Canada)
Translated by Muguraş Maria Vnuck,
(Romania, U.S.A.)

By November, the first day,
Lots of people, hug in cheer
Canada, from far and wide,
In excitement and in joy

In a chaos of mixed colors
Day by day and holiday,
Halloween is giddiness
Both for grown-ups and for kids

Dracula is everywhere,
Masks from phantoms' other world,
Great variety of ghosts
Now display their large fangs.

A great hubbub goes around,
Groups of children everywhere
Knock at doors and knock at gates
Being offered fruits and cakes

I can feel the Christmas carols
Coming out from huge fur caps
'Cause this world is being packed
With all sorts of tales and riddles

أضاعتْ مفاتيحَ رغبتها

علي الحازمي ، السعودية

أنثى وحيدة
تُصارعُ سوطَ الخريف بكفّين عاريتين
من الحظّ والأمل والأصدقاء
الخريف الذي ظلّ يسطو على شجرٍ خبّأتهُ
بعيداً عن العابرين

كم تخافُ من الأمس
من حلمٍ لا يعودُ إلى نومها مرّتين ،
كلّما سيّجتْ بقليل اليدين
فراشات فجرٍ يلوحُ لها
راحَ كفُّ الغياب يُبدّدُ أطيافَها في المهبّ

لم تَعُدْ تكترثْ
لارتحال الحساسين عن ليل شُرفتها
علّمتها الحياةُ بأنْ تنثني عن مباهج فتنتها باكراً
بألا تمدّ يديها إلى ثمرٍ ناضجٍ في غصون الجسد
بألا تُحاول إيقاظَ رعشتها في انحدار المساء ،
أضاعتْ مفاتيحَ رغبتها
في تُخوم انتظارٍ تُمنّي به طائراً
راحَ ينزفُ من رُوحها

14

SHE LOST THE KEYS TO HER DESIRE
Ali Al Hazmi, Saudi Arabia

A lonely woman
Struggling with the whip of autumn
With hands so bare
Of luck, family, and friends
The autumn which kept creeping over
trees she hid
away from the passers

How she fears the past,
and a dream that doesn't visit her sleep twice.
Whenever she fences with the little of her hands
the butterflies of a dawn waving at her,
the palm of absence
went fading her shadows in the wind

She no longer cares
about the goldfinches fleeing of the dimness of her
terrace
Life has taught her to bend away
from the joyfulness of her femininity, so soon
to not reach for the ripe fruit
On the branches of the body
To not try to awaken her shivers
At the fall of night..
She lost the keys to her desire
In the long await with which she consoles the bird
That bleeds from her soul

BAHARDA SEVİŞMEYE SONE
Ali Günvar, Türkiye

bütün sesler susar akşam dağıtırken heceyi.
bir an, âherli serencamdır uzanmış, sarışın
bahar -sîm göğsünü açtıkça diriltir geceyi-
serin bir güzdür öpüştükçe yanar kor dudağım.

umarsız benliğim uçsuz ve bucaksız bedenin-
de sonsuzlukla seviştikçe, doyulmaz olur aşk.
ve çarşaflardaki ıssız gövdesi titrer. teninin
bağıl sislerden ağan özsuyunu doldurur aşk.

karanfiller gibi cevşenli duvarlar… ve hüzün
yayılmıştır yatağın örtüsüne. lâl ve temiz
-mücellâ saksıda- sessizliği âsûde güzün…

sararmıştır beyazın perdede eşleştiği iz.
muhâldir şimdi melûl uçları gönlümüzün.
ağır, suskun bir ışıktır yine eşleştiğimiz.

SONNET FOR MAKING LOVE IN AUTUMN
Ali Günvar, Turkey

all sounds hush when the evening disintegrates the
blossom.
for a moment burnished consequence lies down in
touch
with blonde spring -revitalizing the night, opening
her bosom-
she's a cool autumn burning my lips as we smooch.

when my helpless self sleeps with her immense
flesh, insatiable and greedy becomes love's maze.
and her lonely body trembles in a trance
as love fills us with the juice flowing through the
haze

walls are shielded with carnations…and gloom
is spread on the bed cover. mute and clean
-in a glazed vase- is the silence of the quiet doom.

paled is the trace where the white color pairs off in
vain
impossible are now the weary tips of our souls. o
spleen…
in a heavy and dumb gleam do we pair off again.

DRZWI
Anna Nasiłowska, Polska

Pory roku się przemieszały
jesień to nic pewnego
albo babie lato
albo od razu zima

Wiek dojrzały to nie starość
druga młodość rozsądniejsza niż pierwsza
choć moi znajomi kłócili się
i godzili w nieregularnym rytmie
o, zmiany klimatu

Tyle jest słów zbyt kategorycznych
jak słowo rozstanie
zbyt radykalnie zatrzaskuje drzwi
jak nazwy chorób wywołujących strach

Nie było więc nazw
tylko
złe wyniki badań
o, mogą się poprawić

Gdy wczoraj zadzwonił do mnie
i powiedział: "Ona odeszła"
w pierwszej chwili nie zrozumiałam
które drzwi się zamknęły
i czy można je otworzyć z powrotem

THE DOOR
Anna Nasiłowska, Poland

Seasons have blended
Autumn is nothing certain
Either Indian summer
Or early winter

Maturity is not senility
Second youth is wiser than the first
Though those I had known fought
And reconciled in irregular rhythm
Oh, change of climate

So many words are to definite
Like the word 'apart'
It shuts the door too definitely
Like names of most fearful diseases

So there were no names
Only bad test results
Oh, those can change

When he called me yesterday
And said 'She left'
I didn't understand at first
Which doors were shut
And if they can be ever opened again

HERBST BLUES

Anna Würth, Deutschland

Ein wenig müde bin ich schon
ist ein Vergehen
in der Luft
der Farbenpracht zum Hohn
der Fluß scheint still zu stehn
und doch schwingt
hinter allem ein warmer klarer Ton

UNTERM SEPTEMBERMOND

Magischer Moment
heimkommen in mein Tipi
der Himmel offen

AUTUMN BLUES – AUTUMN BLISS
Anna Würth, Germany
Translated by Anna Engeln, Germany
and Todd Brown, U.S.A.

I am indeed a little weary
something passing in the air
mocks this colourful splendour
the river standing still
and yet behind all this
vibrates a warm pure note

UNDER THE SEPTEMBER MOON

This magic moment
coming home to my tipi
called by the open sky

ΜΟΝΤΕΡΝΟΙ ΠΤΩΧΟΙ

Αριστέα Παπαλεξάνδρου, Ελλάδα

Ίσως αλλάξει ρότα η ζωή
όταν με το καλό φύγει το καλοκαίρι
Κι αν δεν θυμάσαι τι καιρό έχει εδώ
Σ' το λεν ημερολόγια Σ' το λέω κι εγώ
Είναι μια μέρα θερινή
τέλος Νοέμβρη
με μείον το ταμείον μας
ουχί μόνον χρημάτων
μα ελπίδων, λόγων, τακτικών
τε κι αισθημάτων

Κι ό,τι κοντεύει να συμβεί
ό,τι κοντεύει νά 'ρθει
της χειροτέρας εποχής πικρά συμβάντα
Κι απ' τα πικρά το πιο πικρό
που όλο μικραίνει
η λίστα των συμμάχων μας
που όλο αρρωσταίνει

Και συν η πτώση των τιμών
η αναστολή των πληρωμών
και πτώχευση των πάντων

Μέγιστο κραχ των ποιων τιμών;

Ποιων λόγων
ποιων ελπίδων
 κι αισθημάτων;

Μέγιστο κραχ απ' την αρχή
να ξαναρχίσουν όλα
ν' αλλάξει ρότα η ζωή
νά 'ρθει με το καλό το άλλο
καλοκαίρι
Να 'χουν του κόσμου οι μοναξιές
κάτι να πουν
κάποιον να δούνε

MODERN POOR
Aristea Papalexandrou, Greece
Translation: Yannis Goumas, Greece

Maybe life will change trend
when, all being well, summer ends
And if you can't remember what the weather is like
here
the calendars will tell you, I'll tell you
It's a summery day
end of November
our Insurance Fund almost empty
not only of money
but hopes, words, tactics
and feelings as well

And whatever is about to happen
whatever is in the offing
are bitter incidents of the worse of periods
And of the bitter the bitterest
is the list of our allies that keeps on shrinking
keeps on ailing

Plus a slump in prices
the suspension of payments
and everyone's impoverishment

The great crash of what prices?

What words
what hopes
and what feelings?

A great crash beginning at the beginning
for everything to start again
for life to change trend
for blessed summer to come again
for people's loneliness
to have something to say
someone to see

BUČE LEŽIJO NA POLJU

Barbara Pogačnik, Slovenia

Saje jutra se mešajo z nočjo.
Še hiteči vlak skelijo od poletja pogorela polja.
Buče ležijo polne miru v barvi sonca, ki rdi na
   obzorju.
Kot nestalna angela se pogovarjava
pod arkadami v modrem avtu z odprto streho
Piš sili smetano oblakov skoz prste
Na trdem ležišču prepira
nas vedno prestopajo zvezde
Noč s temno grivo strese pod arkadami in se poda
   na ceste
Na begu jem kamnita jabolčka s fasad v Ljubljani
in angelove solze kot pesek raznaša veter,
a jih kasneje prodajajo v veleblagovnicah.
Šum morjá okoli tvojega
golega pasu, ki se dá samo na pol
v objem – kot pismo.
Buče ležijo na polju,
poletje je zapustilo sadove na tihih prtih
plahe peške skrilo v mesnatem oklepu časa.
Sonce se z golo roko dotakne gozda,
vlak se hipno nagne s tira.

PUMPKINS LYING IN THE FIELD

Barbara Pogačnik, Slovenia
Translated by Ana Jelnikar, Slovenia

The soot of morning mixing with the night.
A rushing train smarts from the summer-burnt
    fields.
Pumpkins are lying filled with peace underneath the
    sun, reddening on the horizon.
As inconstant angels we are having a talk
under the arcades in the blue car with an open roof.
A light breeze is forcing the cream of clouds
    through our fingers.
When we lie on the hard bed of argument,
the stars are stepping over us.
The night shakes its dark mane under the arcades
    and hits the road.
On the run, I am eating the little stone apples from
    the facades in Ljubljana
and the wind is blowing angel`s tears away as
    though they were sand,
sending them to be sold in the supermarkets.
The hum of the sea around your
naked waist, which only half-gives itself
to an embrace – be it a letter.
The pumpkins are lying in the field,
the summer has left its fruits on the quiet table-
    cloths,
hid the timid pits into the fleshy armour of time.
The sun with its bare hand touches the forest,
the train for an instant tilts to the side, off the rails.

AUTUMN CAMOUFLAGE
Barry Stevenson, United Kingdom

Once when we were three
there was a tree, the sun, a house

Divebombered death
with all your blood outrun
I see your sprawling battered snout
snoring in the mud

Once there was a tree
when we were three, the sun, a house

in the wet and flattened marsh
green, silver, grey and brown like you:
Autumn has blended
and turned you into one.

Once there was the sun
a tree, a house and us three

together on your helpless wings
a seesaw of rust from nose to tail,
a big dead fish half eaten
by the autumn wind at Warsash
with its hungry weather

There was a tree, a house, the sun

the piping marsh, our sloshing feet
the belch of oily mud
the creak of wounding metal –

last notes
		in the last war's symphony

when we were three
			and couldn't count.

THE THIRD SEASON
Barry Stevenson, United Kingdom

The wilderness of fern is silent now
the moon above the sea-band burns
the waters when the wind has fallen

A day for echoes; stone cannot hold them
nor much of its life passing forgotten:
grey and brown hadrosaurs
stooping for fish in a lake and
a bird with teeth like little knives
pads on a branch above them croaking
–fan-tail and fore-claws bared for fighting

all afternoon– but no-one will

near where the sea tilts at the Kansas shore
Lazy Kansas by the young Atlantic
green, slenderest of oceans, stills
its distant thunder some miles in;
an ankylosaurus grunts to sleep; stars
like nail-heads rise, the claves of night
cruel their silver in an ancient pattern

But here, today, the first leaves fell
here where the wind has fallen —and
autumn for the first time falling

came into the world.

TERZIANNENIN ŞEHRI

Betül Tarıman, Türkiye

geniş halk bahçesi
aşka yakın duruyor
dayısına çeken çocuklar
ara sıra hüzne bakıyor
babaları evlerin
ütülenmiş mendillerinde
yazılmamış bir şiir

terzi annenin şehri
sandık kokulu rüya
çatılarında aşkçıl kuşlar var
kuşlar serin bir oda gibi
her mevsim güz kokar
bahçe bilir bunu
bahçıvan kıyamete kadar

benim terzim zamandır
duvarları her mevsim giz açar
çalışır şiire çalışır gibi
yağmuru hayra yorar

TAILOR MOM'S CITY
Betül Tarıman, Türkiye
Translated by Hasan Yayan, Türkiye

A large public garden
staying close to love
children looking like their uncle
look at sadness sometimes
fathers of houses
on the unironed hankies
an unwritten poem

tailor mom's city
coffer smell dream
lovebirds on the roof
birds like chilly room
every season smells like fall
garden knows that
and gardener till the day of resurrection

my tailor is time
walls confides every season
works like working on poem
interprets rain favourably

DAS KARTOFFELFEUER
Burkhard P. Bierschenck, Deutschland

Wenn über den Herbstblättern
die Schwalben segeln,
im Mollton über Rost und Asche,
verglimmt der Wunsch
nach Weite, Wärme, Hoffnung.

Wenn die Schwalben weinen,
wenn der Rost das Grün zernagt,
wenn rote Kartoffelfeuer
in der Dämmerung glimmen,
und Asche wird aus Weite, Hitze, Begierde,,

Der friedliche Wind dreht auf,
dann fällt das Herbstlaub wieder,
fegt Rost und Asche in die Form
aus Erde, Wärme, Lust.

THE POTATO FIRE
Burkhard P. Bierschenck, Germany

When the swallows are sailing
over the autumn leaves,
over rust and ashes, a soft tone
of wishes for space, warmth, hope,
is dwindling away.

Then the swallows cry,
and the rust gnaws the green,
when red potato fires
gloom in the dusk,
and become ashes
out of space, heat, desire.

Then the trees finally undress,
peaceful the wind turns to full strength,
sweeps rust and ashes into the mold
made of earth, warmth, lust.

ΦΘΙΝΟΠΩΡΙΝΑ ΦΥΛΛΑ

Χλόη Κουτσουμπέλη, Ελλάδα

Το φθινόπωρο τα δέντρα σ' αναβρασμό.
Ασφυκτικά τυλίγονται οι ρίζες,
στενά παπούτσια σε χορό.
Όλο και πιο καχύποπτα.
Σε συστάδες μεταξύ τους.
Ο κορμός χελώνα που ζαρώνει.
Οι ρυτίδες διατρέχουν τα κλαδιά.
Διάφορες φήμες στην ατμόσφαιρα.
Φουντωτή ουρά
ανάμεσα στους θάμνους.
Τα κυνηγόσκυλα οσμίζονται.
Ολόγυρα σκίουροι ξεψυχούν
τον πρώτο κιόλας χρόνο της ζωής τους.
Το γράμμα σου σε τέλος εποχής.
Η φωτοσύνθεση σταμάτησε.
Δεν γνωρίζω αν, για πόσο ακόμα.
Το φθινόπωρο τα φύλλα σπαρταρούν.
Ο χάρτης επάνω τους αλλάζει.
Η πυξίδα δείχνει προς το χώμα.
Θα τηλεφωνηθούμε για τελευταία φορά.
Κανείς απ' τους δυο μας δεν το ξέρει ακόμα.
Έντεχνα κόβεις τον ομφάλιο λώρο απ' το δέντρο.
Σχεδόν δεν θα καταλάβουμε την πτώση.

AUTUMNAL LEAVES

Chloe Koutsoubelli, Greece
Translated by Anna Koustinoudi, Greece

In autumn the leaves are in turmoil.
Their roots twisting, twining, suffocating,
Like tight shoes worn in a dance.
More and more unsettled with suspicion.
In clusters amongst themselves.
The tree trunk a wrinkling turtle.
Its furrows traversing the branches.
Diverse rumours hanging in the air.
A bushy tail
protruding from the bushes.
The hounds picking up the scent.
All around squirrels breathing their last
in their very first year of life.
Your letter out of season now.
Photosynthesis has ceased.
I know not whether or for how long.
In autumn the leaves quiver and throb.
The pattern of their veins constantly changing.
The compass points towards the earth.
We shall call each other for one last time.
Neither of us knows this yet.
Skilfully, you cut off the umbilical cord from the
tree.
We shall barely feel the fall.

HERBSTMOND
Christine Geweke, Deutschland

einsam die straßen und du tanzt tango
mit den herbstblättern im wind. arm in arm
drehen sie sich und du drehst dich um den
eigenen mittelpunkt. alles dreht sich

um die erde, die dich festhält und jedes blatt
jede dunkle berührung ein neuanfang ein
versprechen aus vergangenen zeiten: lebe
tanze und sei führende oder geführter

AUTUMN MOON
Christine Geweke, Germany
Translated by Benjamin Geweke, Germany

deserted streets and you dance tango
autumn leaves in the air, arm in arm
spiraling each other and you circle
around yourself, everything spins

along the earth pulling you and every leave
every dark touch a new beginning
promises from bygone ages: breath
dance and become a leader or follower

HAZAN DER Kİ: BIRAK YAĞSIN
Cigdem Hicran Yorgancioglu, Türkiye

Eril aklın iğdiş ettiği insanlık , aynı kafayla, dişinin
   yaratıcılığını zedeleyerek zimmetine geçirme
   arzusunda katılaştırdı İnsanı.
Tabiatın doğasına patronluk taslamak,
Küresel ısınmayla "New Age " yeni bir sonbahar
   inşa ediyor
Ve bu, yüreğin soğuk tankında hayatı dondurmakta!
Sahte isyankâr ruh haliyle, İnsan betona dönüşüp
   sertleşti
Ezildiğinde toprak sertleşir
Ezilenlerin dünyasında , ezildiğinde İnsan, sertleşir

Vakit bu demdir ,Dünya'nın masumiyeti üzerine
   düşen Asit yağmurunun önünü kesmek için
Göktarlanın göbeğine sözlerimden şiiir tohumlarını
   atmanın zamanı geldi.
Hasat mevsimi geldi .
Bulutların peşinden koşarken rüzgar,
o kovalamacada
Bir kile şekil veren ve hayatı adeta "bir oyun"
   adleden İnsana.
soruveriyor sorusunu düşen Sonbahar yaprakları
"Ala sen söyle nedir Küre-I Arzı derin bir mezarın
   dibine batırıp gömen şey ?"
Cevap ,Her biri ya kurban ya da sahte cesur olan
   sokaklarda kaybolmuş kimliklerin dudaklarından
   dökülüyor .
Aslında Biz ,harika bir bahçede Düşler Ülkesi'nin
   taslak tasarımlarını hayal ediyorduk.

Sonra Dünya'yı lastik bitkileri ve plastik toprakla
örtülü ve sarılı halde bulduk.
Dedi . Beton gökdelen kulelerinin ormanında kay-
bolup sürüklenmiş İnsan
Sahte güç peşinde koşan o iktidarsız ve açgözlü
iştahıyla .

Toprak, sonbahar esintisiyle flört eden derin bir
nefesi içine çeker
Hazan der ki: "Yağmur yağsın !, bırak yağsın da
Küstah kibrin, hakikatin şeffaflığı üzerindeki ka-
ra lekeri uzaklaşabilsin"

AUTUMN SAYS: "LET IT RAIN"
Cigdem Hicran Yorgancioglu, Turkey

Emasculated, dehumanized humanity is born due to
    masculine mind.
That embezzled the female creativity, solidified the
    Human
Patronizing the Nature of the Nature
Constructing a "new age" autumn with global
    warming.
And that makes the life frozen in the cold tank of
    heart!
With fake rebellious mood, Man became concrete
When it crushes, the soil becomes harder.
In the world of the oppressed, when it crushes
    Human becomes hard.

In order to block the acid rain falls on the innocence
    of World
This is the time to throw the seeds of my word into
    a poem in the midst of Sky field harvest season
    came
The wind chasing the clouds away, the falling
    leaves of Autumn asks the question
To the Man, who gives shape to a clay, and fanta-
    sizes life, as "a play"
"What makes the Earth being sunk to a deep grave?,
The reply comes from the lips of identities that are
    lost on the streets,
Each pretending they are either victim or fake brave

Actually we were dreaming the sketch designs of
Wonderland in a gorgeous garden.
But We found earth is being wrapped with rubber
    plants and plastic soil, they call its a   cover.
Said. the drifted Man lost in a forest of concrete
    skyscraper tower.
With his impotent greedy appetite for pseudo
    power.

The soil take a deep breath of life that flirts with
    autumn breeze
Autumn says: "Let It Rain, Let the black spots of
    arrogance will be swiped away from the
    transparency of reality"

LE RUNE D'AUTUNNO
Claudia Piccinno, Italia

Svelate le rune
della saggezza,
definiti i contorni
del tempo,
non m'incute timore
l'autunno.

Lo aspettavo
come ineludibile
incontro
che stempera
i bollori dell'estate
e ci prepara
al gelo.

THE RUNES OF AUTUMN
Claudia Piccinno, Italy

Unveiled the runes
of wisdom,
defined the contours of
time,
the autumn.
does not fear me.

I was waiting for him
as ineluctable
meeting
which dissolves
the boiling of the summer
and makes us ready
to welcome the frost.

AUTUNNO A ROMA
Deborah D'agostino, Italia

Ascolta in lontananza:
non è il fluire delle auto
forse la rincorsa delle onde?
Non è questo boato continuo
simile al rumore del mare?
Comprendi allora i gabbiani
di città, cullati dalla nenia
del traffico, ipnotizzati
dal grigio asfalto.
Hanno scelto il loro mare,
tra questi scogli moderni,
continuano a gridare.
Ascolta bene: non sono
corvi striduli ma canti,
canti di gabbiani.

AUTUMN IN ROME

Deborah D'agostino, Italy

Listen in the distance:
is not the flow of traffic
like the racing waves?
Is not this continuous roaring like
the sound of the sea?
Now you understand the city
seagulls, rocked by the lullaby
of traffic, hypnotized
by the grey asphalt.
They have chosen their sea,
among these modern cliffs,
continuing to cry out.
Listen well: these are
not shrilling crows but songs,
songs of seagulls.

CUNOAŞTERE
Dorel Cosma, România

În contemplarea ce absoarbe
un spate curbat
potoleşte gândurile.
Aduce calmul,
liniştea.
Universul capătă unitate.
Lumea ideilor
ce se prind în
lanţul de mire.
În undele cristaline
rutina se smulge
spre calea deschisă
prin piatră.
O cunoaştere re deschide.
Fiinţă fluidică
în aerul mişcător,
scânteie crescută la văpaie,
insulă cu priviri aţintite
în ceaţă
coloane în câmpul universal
al cunoaşterii

KNOWLEDGE
Dorel Cosma, Romania
Translated by Zorin Diaconescu, Romania

The contemplation consumes
a bowed back
soothes the thoughts.
Brings peace,
quietness.
The world in context.
Only ideas
are lined up
in a chain of a groom.
The clear waves
deprived of routine
take an open path
through stone.
Knowledge becomes apparent.
Flowing creatures
in moving air,
Sparks have grown to flames
an island watching
through fog
the pillars of the universal field
of knowledge.

DIRILIŞ
Emel Koşar, Türkiye

kısaydı renklerin ömürleri
kanatlanıp uçmak için

aşkları aynalarda aradılar
camdan sonbahar ayinleri
sahnelenen
yaseminleri çürüttü
hoyrattı
dirilişin dudakları
utanç akşamları renkleri
örttü
kısaydı...

RESURRECTiON
Emel Koşar, Turkey
Translated by Yaprak Damla Yıldırım, Turkey

too short were the lives
of colors to fly away

they looked for love in mirrors
the vitreous autumn rituals
on the stage
withered the jasmines
coarse
were the lips of resurrection
the nights of shame veiled
the colors
too short…

AN EINEN DEUTSCHEN FREUND

Emina Kamber,
Bosnien und Herzegowina/Deutschland

Ein Mondstrahl weilt
Durch die kleinen Fensterscheiben
Auf meinem Arbeitstisch
So hell und so ungeheuer klar
Ich fühle angestaute Wünsche
In mir
Vom Herbst zum Herbst

In den Augen des Mondes
Verschwommene Bilder
Von damals
Doch das Licht auf meinem Haar
Hofft
Dich
Nicht eines Tages im Herbst
Aufgeben zu müssen

Im Sinne meines Lebens in der Fremde
Von Jahr zu Jahr

TO A GERMAN FRIEND
Emina Kamber, Bosnia and Herzegovina/Germany
Translated by Barry Stevenson, United Kingdom

A moonbeam lingers
Through the little window panes
On my desk, dwells
So bright and so immensely clear
I feel my wishes swell
Within
From fall to fall

In the eyes of the moon
Vague images
From those times before
But its light on my hair
Hopes
I won't have to leave you
In the years to come –

You from my life abroad
– One day in the fall

SONBAHARLA ANIŞMAK
Ertuğrul Özüaydın, Türkiye

Bir uçtan sıkıntılarına koştum şunca aşkla
sofrana kuru ekmeği taşıdım uzun yıllar
uzaklığına ulaştım denize doğru düşe kalka
yan yana yaşantımız karşılığı başka ne ki
senin için düşündüm kendimi hep seninle
en olmazı gizleyen taş sabrıydı içim
bildiklerimse kulağına gümüş küpelerdi

Üçün içinden beşi çıkarınca gördüm de
yarısı sen yarısı seninle geçen ömrümdü
daha fazlasını bölüşmeliyiz günahın
sorunum başka başka anlaşılmasın
hepi topu bu sevinçle yaşadım

Sokak ışıkları oldum korkuna korkarak
düşen pırıltıları topladım uzun hayatlara
kendi ellerimle bıraktım evine son baharı
o akşama dünümüzü bugünümüzü verdim
olacağım ne varsa oldum baştan çıkartan
sonbahar yağmurları, ocak şubat karları
şimdi rüzgârını bekleyen mektup gibiyim

Bu ancak seninle olabilecek yanlışımdı
yine değişemem dünyayı bağışlasalar
bil ki yüreğimdir sende kalan aklım

TALKING ABOUT EACH OTHER

Ertuğrul Özüaydın, Turkey
Translated by Mesut Şenol, Turkey

I hurried to deal with your troubles from one end with
   so much love
for years I brought dry bread to you dinner table
I reached your far-away-ness in fits and starts towards
   the sea
it was about our living side by side, what else could
   its turn be like
I have thought about myself for you, and myself
   always with you
my inner world used to be a stone's patience hiding
   the most impossible
What I knew was simply a lesson I was taught

I noticed something as I was getting three out of five
half was you, and the other half was my life I spent
   with y ou
we should share more of the sin
do not take my question different
overall, my life was ecstatic

I became street lamps by fearing your fear
I collected fallen sparkles for long lives
I took the autumn to its house with my own hands
I gave that evening yesterday and today of ours
I became something whatever is there to seduce
the rain of Autumn, January and February snow
now I am just like a letter waiting for its breeze

This was something to happen only with you
I cannot change even though I am granted the world
just keep in your mind that my mind stuck in you
    happens to be my heart

مِنْ ثُقبِ البَاب

فتحي ساسي   الجمهورية التونسية

في حديقة منزلي،
تلتقي كلُّ الأشجار...
هاربةً منْ لغة الظلّ،
وعلى حافة الورد تُشعلُ رغيفَ العطر.
ثمَّ تجلسُ حولَ طاولة لتتبادلَ الحديث،
وتشربُ أصيصاً على نخب الرّيح.
الفأسُ ينظرُ إليهم خلسةً منْ ثُقب البَاب.   كانت شجرةُ
الخريف حزينةً تبكي،
لأنَّ ورقةً اختنقتْ حين سقطتْ في بركة ماءٍ،
لتشربَ المطرَ...

ON THE PEEPHOLE
Fethi Sassi, Tunisia

In my garden,
all the trees meet each other ...
Fugitive from the shadow language ,
and on the edge of the roses they ignites the loaf of
   perfume.
Sit around a table to share the conversation ,
and drink a stick on the wind toast ...
The ax looks at them stealthily from the peephole.
The autumn tree were sad and crying ,
because a leave choked when it fell in a water pool
to drink water ...

HERBSTMORGEN
Gino Leineweber, Deutschland

Vorhänge filtern
Den Novembermorgen

Dämmernd zerschmilzt
Eine Schneeflocke
An einem warmen Tag
Mein Traum

Sie zittert ein wenig
Als sie zu mir kommt
Bis Lust sich
In ihrem Leib verbreitet

Erwachend bahnt sie sich
Ihren Weg zurück
Zu ihrem Bett
Mein Traum

AUTUMN MORNING
Gino Leineweber, Germany
Translated by Barry Stevenson, United Kingdom

Curtains filter
The november morning

Dawning
A snowflake melts
On a warm day
My dream

She trembles a little
When she comes to me
Until desire
Spreads through her body

Waking up
She takes her leave
Back to – her bed
My dream

BÖYLE RÜZGÂRLAR
Gonca Özmen, *Türkiye*

Böyle şeyler oluyor işte böyle rüzgârlar
Bu güz balkonu beni çağırıyor

Neyi dağıtıyor elin akşamda
Ben saçlarımı topluyorum ırmakları da

Sonra gidip bir şiirin önünde soyunuyorum
Bir çocuğu öpüyorum adı sevişmek oluyor

Her şey bizden ayrı
Her şey biz varken yan yana oluyor

Bu oluşa biraz keder ekliyorum

Ellerinde bir ağaç
Ellerinde telaşlı bir ağaca bakıyorum

Sen oturup şeftali yiyorsun
Otlar diyorum yürüyor görmüyorsun

Sıkıntılı bir yağmur geçiyor pencerelerden
Kendime sesleniyorum ses vermiyor

Ah sevgilim aramızda bir iğne
Beni sana dikiyor

WINDS LIKE THESE
Gonca Özmen, Turkey
Translated by George Messo,
United Kingdom

These things happen, winds like these
   This autumn balcony calls me
Whatever your hands dispense at night
   I gather up my hair and rivers too
Then I go and undress in front of a poem
   I kiss a child its name becomes love
Everything is distant from us
   When with us, nothing is alone
I accent a little sorrow to this presence
There's a tree in your hands
   I'm looking at a bustling tree in your hands
You sit, eating a peach
   Grass is walking, I say, don't you see
Oppressive rain passes the window
   I call out to myself, there's no reply
O my love, there's a needle between us
   Stitching me to you

ਪੂਰਾ ਚੰਨ

ਗੁਰਿੰਦਰ ਸਿੰਘ ਕਲਸੀ

ਤੂੰ ਮੇਰੇ ਪਿਆਰ ਦਾ ਸਿਖਰ ਹੈਂ
ਤੈਥੋਂ ਪਹਿਲਾਂ
ਮੈਂ ਕਈਆਂ ਨੂੰ ਪਿਆਰ ਕੀਤਾ
ਕੁਝ ਨੇ ਮੇਰੇ ਨਾਲ ਫੁੱਲ ਵੰਡੇ
ਕੁਝ ਨੇ ਕੰਡੇ
ਕੁਝ ਨੇ ਪੈਸੇ ਅਤੇ ਵੰਡੇ ਤੋਹਫੇ
ਕੁਝ ਨੇ ਬਸ ਮੁਸ਼ਕਿਲਾਂ
ਪਰ ਤੂੰ ਮੇਰੇ ਨਾਲ ਵੰਡੀ ਪੂਰੀ ਜ਼ਿੰਦਗੀ
ਬਿਨਾ ਕਿਸੇ ਸੰਗ ਝਿਜਕ ਦੇ
ਤੂੰ ਮੈਨੂੰ ਮੁਕਤ ਕਰ ਦਿੱਤਾ
ਹਰ ਇਕ ਹੱਦ ਤੋਂ

ਤੂੰ ਮੇਰੇ ਪਿਆਰ ਦਾ ਸਿਖਰ ਹੈਂ
ਭਵਿੱਖ ਵਿਚ
ਮੈਂ ਸੋਚਦਾ ਹਾਂ
ਕਿ ਮੈਨੂੰ ਰੁਕ ਜਾਣਾ ਚਾਹੀਦਾ ਹੈ
ਮੈਨੂੰ ਕਿਸੇ ਨੂੰ ਵੀ ਸੱਦਣਾ ਨਹੀਂ ਚਾਹੀਦਾ
ਪਿਆਰ ਕਰਨ ਲਈ
ਮੈਨੂੰ ਤੇਰੇ ਪਿਆਰ ਨਾਲ
ਰੱਜ ਜਾਣਾ ਚਾਹੀਦਾ ਹੈ
ਤੇਰਾ ਪਿਆਰ ਮੇਰੀ ਜ਼ਿੰਦਗੀ ਦਾ
ਪੂਰਾ ਚੰਨ ਹੈ
ਤੂੰ ਮੇਰੇ ਪਿਆਰ ਦਾ ਸਿਖਰ ਹੈਂ ।

***

THE FULL MOON
Gurinder Singh Kalsi , India

You are the top of my love
Before you
I loved many people
Some shared the flowers with me
Some shared the thorns with me
Some shared money and gifts
Some shared only problems
But you
Shared the whole life with me
Without any hesitation
You made me free
From all boundaries

You are the top of my love
In future , I think
I should stop now
I should not invite others to love me
I should be satisfied by your love
Your love is the full moon of my life
You are the top of my love.

SONBAHAR AKŞAMI
Hilal Karahan, Türkiye

Dikkatle sıvazlar göbeğini zamanın
siğilli elleriyle sessizlik
akşam olmaktan yorulmuş
güne sofra kurar

İnciler dökülmüş tarlalara
bulutların yeni bağlanmış uçkurundan

Gün boyu koşturmuş toprak
kayalığa mı takılıp düşmüş
obadan ovaya?
dizleri çamur, ay tozu, safran

Anlayamaz bir başına taşların
içini usul usul oyanı:
ne dans eden otlar
ne gerinen çalılık
ne de ayak izlerini koklayan rüzgâr

AUTUMN EVENING
Hilal Karahan, Turkey

Carefully patting paunch of time
the silence with warty hands
prepares table for the tired day
to turn into evening

Pearls are poured on the fields
from recently tied waistband of clouds

Rushing all day, has the earth
stuck to the cliff and fallen down
from brae to meadow?
her knees are mud, moon dust, saffron

What scoops out alone stones
none of them can understand:
dancing grass,
stretching thicket,
or the wind smelling footprints

AFTER THE FALL
Holly Iglesias, U.S.A.

1. ROSEMARY

I remember you like I remember the coming of cold,
slow and dull, nothing distinct, no smell attached
nor sound, only a small mark, a pock perhaps or a
fading bruise. Hardly worth remarking upon, or
rubbing to ease the pain.

If I remember the cold, or you, at all, it is as a
drowsy slog up that closed staircase, a puritanical
contrivance with tall risers, splinters at the edge of
shallow treads snagging my wool socks.

If I remember impending winter in the farmhouse
that delighted you so, with its knob-and-tube wiring
and stripped window sashes, it is as the suffocation
of window quilts, heavy patterns in rust and plum
blocking what little light remained.

2. MONSTERA DELICIOSA

I remember you like I remember the machete under
the mattress. The belt tossed over a chair. Your hand
cocked to slap.

If I remember the heat, or you, at all, it is episodic,
brief, a fierce, fleeting palpitation that warned of
deeper troubles.

If I remember the AC set at 65, the maid from Gua-
temala, the leather furniture and crystal barware that
stoked your ego, it is as the girl holding her breath
at the bottom of the pool, pages torn from her diary
floating to the surface.

БИ НАМАР

Женни Лхагвасүрэн, Монгол

Зүрх минь намрын навчны хэлбэртэй
Сэтгэл минь намрын үзэсгэлэнгийн дайтай
Нүд минь намрын тэнгэр шиг тунгалаг
Би тэр чигээрээ намар
Дуулах минь намрын шувуудын ганганаа
Бүжих минь намрын хонгор салхи
Нулимс минь намрын шаагих бороо
Би тэр чигээрээ намар
Тэртээ намрын уулнаас
Тэнгэрийн уянга эгшиглэнэ
Тэнд намар болсон би
Хөгжим тоглож суугаа

I AM AUTUMN
Jenny Lkhagvasuren, Mongolia

My heart is in the shape of an autumn leaf
My soul is like autumn beauty
My eyes are clear as autumn sky
I am autumn
My song is autumn birds' crackle
My dance is autumn wind
My tears are autumn rain
I am autumn
From the far mountain of autumn
A melody of Heaven is sounding harmoniously
There, I who turned into autumn
Am playing now joyfully

AUTUMNAL
Juan C. Tajes, Uruguay

En mi antes la noche era más noche,
Los fantasmas se asustaban de si mismos,
La sombra era la sombra de la luna
Y las estrellas caían en la nada.

En este ahora mis padres fermentan en el seno de la
tierra,
Humos, raíz y turba.
Desde su invierno preparan mi otoño,
Último coletazo de la melancolía
Que exhala el aroma del ocre.

Una primavera nos fuimos a la lucha,
Mano en mano.
Este otoño los recuerdos son hongos
Entre la hojarasca,
Líquen y musgo en la piedra quieta.
Recuerdos inventados, como todos,
O la ausencia del recuerdo.

No te pido que me creas,
Sólo quiero que me escuches
Sin verificar mis voces ni mis ecos,
Que no cierres los ojos
Cuando te adentres en las arboledas
Adonde la madera canta en la voz de la marimba,
Adonde le responde el silbido del viento
Que depista a los ciegos,
Mientras duerme la semilla su orgasmo germinal.

AUTUMNAL
Juan C. Tajes, Uruguay

In my before the night was more night,
The phantoms were scared of themselves,
The shadow was the shadow of the moon
And the stars fell into nothingness.

In this now my parents ferment in the bosom of the
earth,
Humus, root and peat.
From their winter they prepare my autumn,
Last lash of melancholy
That exhales the scent of ocher.

One spring we went to the struggle,
Hand in hand
This autumn our memories are like mushrooms
Among the leaf litter,
Lime and moss on the still stone.
Invented memories, like all of them,
Or the absence of memory.

I'm not asking you to believe me,
I just want you to listen to me
Without verifying my voices or my echoes,
Do not close your eyes
When you go into the groves
Where the wood sings in the voice of the marimba,
Where the wind whistle
That mislead the blind, responds,
While the seed sleeps its germinal orgasm.

ALCANTARILLAS
Julio Pavanetti, Uruguay/España

Cada hoja sacudida por un árbol que tiembla,
cada luz que agoniza orillando el silencio,
cada paso que doy y crecen mis quimeras,
cada ruta hacia el túnel que me lleva a lo inverso,
cada día que pasa respiro más ausencias
cuyo recuerdo escolta mi penúltimo vuelo.

Soy un soplo sin aire ahogado en el espejo,
otoño consumiéndose como el sol en el río.
Soy un sueño crepúsculo que escala hacia el descen-
so,
un charco diluido en el cemento arrítmico
brotando de los ojos más cansados del tiempo.
Soy los bordes cautivos del viaje hacia el abismo.
¿Cómo enfrentar la vida que se escurre sin tregua
por las alcantarillas que las noches engendran?

SEWERS
Julio Pavanetti, Uruguay/Spain

Each leaf shaken by a trembling tree,
each light that agonizes bordering the silence,
every step I take feeding my chimeras,
each way towards the tunnel that leads me in oppo-
site direction,
every day I breathe more absences
whose memory escorts my penultimate fluttering.

I'm a breathless air drowned in the mirror,
autumn consuming like sun in the river.
I am a twilight dream that climbs towards the de-
scent,
a puddle diluted in the arrhythmic cement
sprouting from the most tired eyes of time.
I am the captive edges of the journey into the abyss.
How to face the life that flows without respite
by the sewers that nights engender?

ΛΙΆΝΑ ΣΑΚΕΛΛΊΟΥ

Η άλλη όψη της γλώσσας, Ελλάδα

Έχει εγκαταλείψει το ξέχειλο καταύγασμα
της άνοιξης και μπαίνει στον κήπο
για να παλέψει με την συμπιεσμένη σκληρότητα
των νοημάτων.

Ο θόρυβος από τις άλλες ζωές κρύβεται
στη σιωπή του φθινοπώρου.
Οι σφήκες σαρώνονται, τα μήλα μωλωπίζονται,
το σηρικό μαντήλι πιάνεται σ' ένα κλαδί
κι αιωρείται με την κίνηση της σκέψης.

Κατευθύνει τη μουσική από το νεύρο στη φωνή
σμιλεύοντας την ενέργεια
με το αεικίνητο εργαλείο
της λεπτουργίας της.

Αυτή η γενναιότητα προς το βάρος της ζωής
έρχεται με καθυστέρηση. Τα μήλα, το μαντήλι,
οι σφήκες καταφθάνουν σαν λυπητερός σκοπός.
Ζει πέρα απ' το λεπτό, πτερώνει την
    παρόρμησή της,
μονολογεί, η αληθινή τέχνη δεν οξειδώνεται.

THE OTHER SIDE OF LANGUAGE
Liana Sakelliou, Greece

She has abandoned the overflowing glare
of spring and enters the garden
to struggle with the compressed harshness
of meanings.

The noise from other lives is concealed
in autumn's silence.
The wasps are swept away, the apples bruise,
the silk scarf catches on a branch
and sways with the movement of thought.

She directs the music by the verve in her voice
chiseling the energy
with the restless tool
of her delicate work.

This courage faced with life's burden
comes with delay. The apples, the scarf,
the wasps arrive like a sad refrain.
She outlives the moment, gives wing to her
  impulse,
soliloquizes, true art does not rust.

ΕΠΟΧΙΚΌ

Λίλυ Εξαρχοπούλου, Ελλάδα

Το φθινόπωρο είναι σαν τη μητέρα μου
Γήινο, άφυλλο και λυπημένο
Προετοιμάζεται για τα χειρότερα
Κοιτώντας τον Χάρο στα μάτια

Ο χειμώνας είναι σαν τον πατέρα μου
Χιονισμένες δειλές συναντήσεις και
Πουντιασμένες μοναχικές νύχτες
Βίαιες καταιγίδες και απέραντη ησυχία

Η άνοιξη είναι σαν τον μικρό μου αδελφό
Κεφάτη, ανάλαφρη, ανόητη
Υποδέχεται την ενηλικίωση με ριγέ γραβάτα
Αδημονώντας να προϋπαντήσει την κοπέλα του

Το καλοκαίρι μοιάζει με εμένα στις καλές μου
Υπεροπτικό, αστόχαστο, ηλιοκαμμένο
Σούζι Κιου στην καρδιά, Αθηνά στη σοφία
Αλλοπρόσαλο, αδιάλλακτο, επιφανειακό

Τι χρονιά κι αυτή, τι οικογένεια!

SEASONAL
Lily Exarchopoulou, Greece

Autumn is like my ma
Earthly, leafless and sad
Preparing for the worst
Looking the Grim Reaper in the eye.

Winter is like my daddy
Snowy timid encounters
Chilly lonely nights
Fierce storms and infinite quietness

Spring is like my little brother
Buoyant, surprising, silly
Welcoming adulthood with a tie
Leaning on the windowsill for his lass.

Summer is like me at my best
Arrogant, thoughtless, sunburned
Susie Q in the heart, Minerva in the intellect
Whimsical, intolerant, vain.

What a year, what a family!

NEUE BÄUME
Maren Schönfeld, Deutschland

Euch sehen, Bäume
in Gelb und Rot
das leise Rascheln des Fallens
wie leicht mein Gang durchs Laub
und das Aufsammeln
besonders schöner Blätter

Meine früheren Bäume
in der Stille des Novembermorgens
allein am Elbufer, und ich
bei ablaufend Wasser nicht mehr
den ganzen Weg am Strand zurück

Euch suchen, neue Bäume
in meinem kleiner gewordenen
Schrittkreis finden, irgendwie
die Meditation des Gehens
ohne Wanderung

NEW TREES
Maren Schönfeld, Germany
Translated by Barry Stevenson, United Kingdom

Looking at you
trees in yellow and red
in the soft rustle of your fall,
how easy my way through the foliage
and the choice of beautiful leaves

My one-time trees
of a still November morning
alone on the banks of the Elbe, and I
no longer by ebbtide return
my way along the shore

Looking for you, new trees,
yet finding somehow
in my more confined space
the meditation of walking bereft
of the freedom to wander so far

IK BEN EEN JONGEN MET AUTISME
Marian Ekelhof, Nederland

Kijk me niet langer in de ogen dan enkele seconden
genoeg om je verborgen agenda's,
dubbele moraal en opgekropte emoties te door-
   gronden,
de subtiele ondertoon van onvermogen in je stem,
netjes verpakt in schorre regenbogen
ik tel een voor een voor een onbeantwoorde
   dromen
in de duistere spiegels van je ziel.

ook al delen we alleen de bank
praten we niet: ik en jij.

Kijk me niet onnodig lang in mijn ogen, ik ontplof,
vernietig alles op mijn weg zonder mededogen.

Vol tederheid, wanhoop, klopt mijn hart,
duw me niet over de grens
ook al kijk ik niet op dezelfde manier tegen de ding-
   en aan
ga er anders mee om,
niet om jou te kwetsen, niet om jou pijn te doen.

Wanneer je mijn structuur saboteert
met hondenstront op je schoenen en onverschil-
	ligheid
alle grenzen overtreedt, dan zie je me niet meer
	terug,
zelfs in een verafgelegen universum kom je me
	nergens tegen.
Mijn liefde is niet zilver
Mijn hart is goud, echt en onevenwichtig,
Ik ben een jongen met autisme.

I AM AN AUTISTIC BOY
Marian Ekelhof, The Netherlands

It will be enough for me
look into your eyes,
so full of unexpected emotions,
for only a few seconds
in order to observe the turmoil
deep within,
discover it's multiple disorder disguises,
hidden agendas and untold secrets
amidst the dark mirrors of your goals.

So very tender is the soft embrace of
your presence even when we share only the couch,
even though we don't talk.

Don't look me in the eye
for a length of time
I will explode feeling powerless
without warning
In whatever context, randomness
I'll destroy all on my way
Full of tenderness
yet desperate
don't push me over the edge
my beloved guide
I might have other ways
of looking at things
of coping
not to frustrate you
not to make you feel sad.

If you trespass the boundaries of my structures,
break into my safety zone,
with dogshit all over your shoes
and carelessness,
I'll never come back
not in the farthest universe
You'll see me return.

My love isn't silver
My heart is gold
Real and unstable
I am an autistic boy

ЗАВРЪЩАНЕ
Марина Савова, България

Ухание на есен, на дъжд, на завръщане,
На спомен скъп от минали дни,
На нещо познато, но още неслучило се,
Раждат се нов ден и нови съдби!

Сияние влажно обвива душата ми,
Мъглата е було, но изгряват звезди,
Пътят се вижда - нататък,
След вчера, след днес, след утре дори!

Усещане познато – на неповторимост,
На мигове, които нямат край,
На нещо близко и любимо,
Тих шепот от земния рай!

Сънят ми се сбъдва – притихвам,
Превръща се в думи, дела и мечти,
Пророчество древно бележи живота ми
И нежно ми казва – върви!

Мислите спират, изчезват въпросите,
Само сърцето неспирно шепти:
...и все пак...дали....

COMING BACK
Marina Savova, Bulgaria
Translated by Theodora Burgudzhieva

It smells of autumn, of rain, of coming back,
of precious memories of days past,
of something familiar as yet unfulfilled,
of a new day and new destinies being born.

A humid glow envelops my soul,
The fog is a veil, but the stars are appearing,
there is a road -   that way,
beyond yesterday, beyond today, beyond to-
morrow.

A familiar feeling - of uniqueness,
of moments that have no end,
of something you cherish and love,
a quiet murmur of paradise on earth.

My dream is being fulfilled as – I stand still,
my dream is now words, deeds and reveries,
an ancient prophecy puts a mark on my life
and gently tells me that you go ahead!

No more thoughts, no more questions,
only the heart whispering gently
... and still... is this true?

ALAM MUSIM LURUHKU
Mawar Marzuki, Malaysia

Aku telah mendengar,
tentang musim luruhmu yang indah
daunan meranum hijau, kuning, merah keemasan
menari bagai ballerina tatkala kau bagaikan
berjalan terus ke dalam api
tanpa merasa kepanasan
permaidani keemasan mengelus telapakmu
musim panas dan musim salju bertingkah
mengurniakan angin jemari nakal
yang rakus menanggalkan dedaunan longgar
sehingga pohon berdiri telanjang
dingin, mendepani hari hari mentari malas
sendiri…dan sepi

Tentu
kau juga tidak tahu tentang musim luruhku
di mana aku pernah tinggal
antara pohon-pohon yang ditoreh getahnya
warna-warna hari musim luruhku
secantik warna musim luruhmu
cuma… angin dan panas bercengkerama
meluruhkan daun-daun tua
menanggalkan pohon getah berderet telanjang
Tuhan menghantarkan kami kemarau
telaga dan sungai menjadi tohor
kekadang tedung selar merayap antara daun-daun
    mati

Pohon bermusim itu
membuat aku faham tentang musim luruh
mendengar keluh ibu
beras sudah cangkat diguri
diam bapa tentang kepayahan
merenung jauh deret-deret pohonan yang telanjang
tanpa daun, tanpa darah
hari panjang dan usang
menanti daun muda bertunas

Dan 'pop' meletus biji getah
memberitahu kami
Dia mengirim kemarau
an Dia juga mengirim irama harapan
masa depan

MY DESCIDUOUS DAYS
Mawar Marzuki, Malaysia

I've heard
about your beautiful autumn
leaves   ripen from green to yellow, red and gold
whirling like ballerinas as you walked
straight into a flame
without feeling the heat
carpet of golden leaves caressing your feet
granting the wind   mischievous fingers
rapaciously loosening leaves
till the trees stood naked
and cold, under the days of only sun rays
alone…and lonely

Maybe
you're innocent of my autumn, too
where I once lived
were trees tapped for latex
the colours of my deciduous days
were as beautiful as yours
except that the wind and the heat entangled
shedding old leaves
till the rubber trees stood naked in rows
God sent us drought
wells and rivers shallowing
at times king cobras slithering among the dead
   leaves

Those deciduous trees
made me understood the meaning of autumn
hearing   mother sighed

about rice deep in the guri[2]
and father's musings over meagre
that faraway look in his eyes
and row and rows of naked rubber trees
void of leaves void of milky blood
long, hot obsolete days
waiting for the shoots to sprung
and 'pop' went the rubber seed
telling us
He sends   drought
but He also sends music of hope
the promising song
of future

[2] Guri: big earthenware pot used to keep rice grains

GÜZ YAPRAKLARININ DÜŞME ZAMANI GELDI

Mesut Şenol, Türkiye

Hiç bitmeyen bir döngü, dolaşıyor evreni kusursuz
  kaoslarıyla
İnsanlar, yarı canlı bitkiler – ya da biz öyle düşünüyoruz –
  bizden bile canlı olabilirler
Ayık bir kafa ya da hasta bir ruh – bilinen ya da bilinmeyen
  neyse
İnan bana diyor bilge, yaşlı ve usta bir adam bin bir yüzüyle

Bir şeyleri hayal edebilirsiniz zaman zaman, bazen çok fazla
Umutlar uçar ve bir yerlere konar kimi durumlarda
Güz yaprakları beklenmeyen bir şeylerde bulurlar kendile-
  rini
İster ormanın dibinde isterse sürüklenerek bir rüzgârın
  kanatlarında

Güzün felsefesi nedir ya da o niye durur mevsimlerin
  arasında
Gövdesinin dalları ondan ayrılmayı ister
Yapraklar sanki evi terk eden çocuklar gibi yol gösterir
Onları kurtaracak anneler ve babalar yoktur ama

Haydi, yanı başımıza düşen yaprakları görmemenin bir
  yolunu buluver
Kalp ağrını unutmak için gözlerini kapatmayı
  seçebilirsin
Eğer birisine veda etmek zorunda kalırsan
Orada zaten hazır bekleyen güz mevsimi hemen başlayıverir

HIGH SEASON FOR THE FALL
OF THE AUTUMN LEAVES

Mesut Şenol, Turkey

A never ending cycle, circling the universe with its precise
    chaos
Humans, half-alive plants – or we think so – they might be
    livelier even
A conscious mind or a disturbed soul – what is known or
    not known
Believe me says a wise, an aged and a seasoned man of
    many faces

Imagining things might occur too, at time too many
The hopes fly and land in some instances
Autumn leaves find their place in somewhere
    unexpected
Be it the floor on the forest of a wind's wing to be carried
    away

What is Autumn's philosophy or why is it in between sea-
    sons
The branches of the body want to break up from it
Leaves usher the way as if kids leaving home
There are no moms of dads to come to rescue

Come on find a way not to see the leaves fall
    nearby
You may close your eyes to ignore your heartache
If it ever happens to you to say goodbye to someone
It may start the season of Autumn already there ready…

УНОСИМ У СЕБЕ ОДЈЕК СУНЦА

Милица Јефтимијевић Лилић, Србија

Кад пробудим се, отпоздрављам сунцу
Захвално
Уносим у себе речи молитве
Да прозраче ме светошћу
Прочисте од примеса мрака.
Направе рез да ништа јучерашње
Не дотакне ми срце,
Траг остави гнусних збивања с екрана
Крволочне борбе
Међу председничким кандидатима
Одјеке бомби на светским аеродромима
Измучена лица гладне деце
Што свест ломе
Унезверени погледи мајки
Што узалудно трагају за синовима
Који се нису вратили са ратишта,
Дрске облине старлета
Које испуњавају цео екран,
Еуфоричне салве смеха
Површних водитеља
Заглушујућа бука улице
Крици неуротичних суседа
Што се у општој беспомоћности
Међусобно растржу.
Уносим у душу узвишени мир молитве

Створене у далеким тишинама вере
Да њом подупрта терет дана
Изнесем часно
Без бола, клетве, поклекнућа.
Уносим у себе постојаност сунца
Да одјекне од свега јаче,
Да покушам да опет осветлим моју јесен.

I TAKE INTO MYSELF
THE ECHO OF THE SUN

Milica Jeftimijević Lilić, Serbia
Translated by Lazar Macura, Serbia

When I wake up I wave back to the Sun
Gratefully
I take into myself the words of a prayer to permeate
   me with holiness,
To purge me of the dark,
To make a slash so that nothing of yesterday can
   touch my heart
Or leave traces of henious acts from the screen,
Of bloodthirsty struggle among presidential candi-
   dates,
Of bomb echoes at airports worldwide,
Of tormented faces of hungry children
Disturbing consciounsness,
Of disconcerted gazes of mothers lookin in vain for
   their sons
Who have not come back from the battlefield,
Of impudent rotundities of starlets,
Of euphoric salvoes of laughter of shallow hosts,
Of deafening street noise,
Of screams of neurotic neighbours
Tearing one another apart
In universal helplessness.

I take into my soul the sublime peace of a prayer
Originated in remote silences of faith

In order to honorably carry the burden of the day
Supported by it
Without a pain, curse or bowing knees.
I take into myself the constancy of the Sun
To resound stronger than anything,
To try again to shine my autumn.

EVVEL
Okan Yılmaz, Türkiye

sonbaharlardan dönerken
sıkı sımsıkı bir cinayeti arayan
cebinde sustalı ıssız bir katil gibi
avucuma yazgısını çiziyor
elektrikli elbiseler ve
yedi renkli saçlarla sokaklardayım
tanrım ne güzel ölümlere göz yumuyorsun
üşüyen kedileri saymıyorum bile
bu yılda böylesine protest olacağım
aklımın ucundan geçmezken
hangi sokakta öldürüleceğimi tahmin ediyorum
tecavüzü değil aşkı öteleyen zihinleriniz
siz kara kapkara ressamlar
tuvallerinizde irin
ben o sonbaharlardan dönen aşklarla ıslanırken
kanımızı havaya karıştırmak isteyen vahşi kalabalık
duyumsayın beni
ağlıyorum ağlıyorum ağlıyorum

BEFORE

Okan Yılmaz, Turkey
Translated bv Yasemin Üşümüş, Turkey

while i am turning back from autumns
he who is looking for a tight, very tight a murder
like a deserted murderer who has a switch-blade in
his pocket
he is scracthing my fate to my palm
with electiric dresses
and seven colour hairs, i'm in the street
my lord, how lovely you're shouting your eyes to
the deaths
i'm not even counting the cats which feel cold
in this year, i will be protest like this
while it doesn't even cross my mind
i'm guessing that which street i'm going to be mur-
dered
your minds which exclude love not rape
you, black, pitch-black painters
pus in your canvases
while i was getting wet with the loves which turn
back from those autumns
the brutal crowd who wants to blend our blood to
the air
feel me
i'm crying, crying, crying

GÜZ YALNIZLIĞI
Osman Öztürk, Türkiye

Bir güz yalnızlığı sardı
Yüreğimin arsız dağlarını derinden
Güz yalnızlığı dağ fırtınasından beter
Arayıp sormasan da beni
Uzaklardan bir tebessümün yeter.

Sesin çağlayan ırmağın nağmesi
Sisli gözlerin hayal denizi
Dilin bal damlatan karakovan peteği
Dudağıma bir damla bal akıtsan yeter.

Gönlüm sakinleşmiyor sen yokken
Deli bir rüzgâr sarıyor içimi
Dal dal yapraklarım kururken
Bir kibrit çaksan yanmama yeter.

Gönlüm yayla suları kadar duru ırmağında
Ne bir çöl susuzluğu çatlar dudaklarımda
Ne de bir gam sızlar suskun bağrımda
Bir seher vakti yayla çiçeği gibi açsan
Göğsümde yeter.

Gönlümden geçene yüreğim yetmez
Kördüğüm olur kurduğum saklı cümleler
İçimde donar senden kalan hasretler
İşte o an içli bir dokunuşun yeter.

Bilmesin kimse yüreğimin sana düşkünlüğünü
Sensiz kundakta yetim bir çocuğa döndüğümü
Seninle ağlayıp seninle güldüğümü
Seni öylesine güçlü bir aşkla sevdiğimi
Sadece sen bil yeter.

AUTUMN SOLITUDE

Osman Öztürk, Turkey
Translated by Mesut Şenol, Turkey

An Autumn solitude hugged
Brazen mountains of my heart deeply
Autumn solitude is worse than the mountain gust
Even though you don't show concern for me
One smile on your face would suffice.

Your voice is like gurgling river's melody
Your misty eyes are the sea of fantasy
Your tongue is honey dropping from the natural
  honey comb
Your pouring one drop of honey on my lip would
  suffice.

When you are away, my soul cannot be in peace
A crazy wind fills me
As my leaves were drying like branches
Striking a match would suffice to burn me.

My soul is calm in your clear river like highland
  waters
There is no desert thirst cracking on my lips
Neither a grief stings my silent chest
It would suffice
If you would bloom like a highland flower at one
  dawn
On my chest.

The one in my mind cannot be sufficient for my
  heart
The hidden sentences I made would become
  tangled
Longing left by you freezes inside me
Then your soulful touching would suffice.

Let no one know my soul's fondness for you
Without you, my turning into an orphan child in
  swaddle
My crying and laughing with you
My loving you so strongly
It would suffice if you let yourself know it only.

نَوْرسُ الرُّؤيَا
رائد أنيس الجشي

وَرَأَيْتُ
نَوارسَ تُحَلِّقُ فِيْ رُؤى التَّكَامُلِ
وَتَبْتَكِرُ الصَّهِيلْ

وَرَأيتُ
صَدَقَةَ فُتَاتٍ
تَتَسَاقَطُ مِنْ رَغِيفِهَا المَصْلُوبِ
لِتَعْتَاشَ عَلَيه
الجُرْذَانُ الكَتَبَةُ

وَرَأيتُ
رَفِيفَ جونَ النَّوَارسِ
يَبْتَلِعُ سَمَكَ العُرْفِ
وَيُعِيْدُ تَشْكِيلَ رَقْصِ تَمَائِمِ الفِضَّةِ
عَلَى مُنْحَنَى البَحرْ

وَرَأيتُ
جُرْذَانًا تَتَنَمَّرُ عَلَى انْكِسَارِ الضَّوءِ
وَتَظُنُّ أَنَّهَا مَنْبَعُ الإنَارَةِ
فِيْ الطِّينْ
...

THE ARRIVAL OF SEAGULLS

Raed Anis Al-JIshi, Saudi Arabia
Translation by Amira Rammah, Tunisia

I have seen gulls,
in holy visions,
hover and invent
the sound of horses.

I have seen them
give alms to rats
hungry for crumbs of bread,
crucified on the altar.

I have seen them
flap their wings and swallow
common rules of fish.
Reinvent the physics
of a silver talisman's dance
on the sea's curve.

I have seen rats
feast at the fall of dusk.
They claim to be the genesis of light.

ಶರತಋಋರಾಲ

ರಶರ್ಮರಾ ರಮರೇಶರ್, ಭರಾರತ

ಶರತರ್ಕರಾಲ ನರೀ ಪಂಪರೋರರ್ನಲರ್ಲಿರಯವ ಕರೇಸರಿ
    ಹೂಂವಯಂಗಳಂತರೆಯರೇ ಅಂದವರೇ?
ಅಥವರಾ ಕರಾಶರ್ಮರೀರದ ಚರೆನರ್ನರಾರರ್ ಚರೆಲರ್ಲಯವ
    ಎಲರೆಗಳ ಹರಾಗರೆ ನರೀ ಹಳದರಿಯರೇ?
ನರೀ ಕಡಯಂಗರೆಂಪಯ ಮರೇಲರಾವರಣದಡಿ ನರಿನರ್ನ
    ಬರ್ಕೈಸರಿಕಲರ್ ಸವರಾರಿ
    ಮರಾಡರ್ಡಯಂತರ್ತರಿರಯವರೆಯರಾ?
ಅಥವರಾ ದರಾಲಿನ ನರೀಲರಿ ನರೀರರಿನಲರ್ಲರಿ ದರೋಣರಿ
    ಹರಾಯಯಂತರ್ತರಿದರಿಯರೇ?
ನರೀನಯ ಧರರ್ಮಶರಾಲರಾದ ಪರರ್ವತಗಳರೊಂದರಿಗರೆ
    ಮರಾಡರ್ಡಯಂತರ್ತರಿರಯವರೆಯರಾ?
ಲಥಖರ್ನಲರ್ಲಿನ ಹಳದರಿ ಮರಗಳರಿಂದ
    ಬಂದರ್ಧನನರ್ನಯ ಕರೆಮರಾಡಯಂತರ್ತರಿದರೀಯರಾ?
ಮರೆಯರಾಗಯಂತರ್ತರಿರಯವ ಮರ್ಯರಾಪಲರ್ ಎಲರೆಗಳ
    ಮರೇಲರೆ ಕವರಿತರೆಗಳನರ್ನಯ
    ಬರರೆಯಯಂತರ್ತರಿರಯವರೆಯರಾ?
ನರೀ ನರೆರಳರಿಲರ್ಲದ ಅಕರ್ಟರೋಬರರ್ ಬರಾನನರ್ನಯ
    ನರೋಡಯಂತರ್ತರಿರಯವರೆಯರಾ?
ಅಥವರಾ ಬರೀಳಯವ ಎಲರೆಗಳ
    ತಲರೆತರಿರಯಂಗಯವರಿಕರೆಯರಿಂದ
    ಚರೇತರಿಸರಿಕಗೊಳಯಂತರ್ತರಿರಯವರೆಯರಾ?
ಶರತರ್ಕರಾಲ ನರೀನಯ ಎಷರ್ಟಯ ಚರೆನರ್ನರಾಗರಿ ನನರ್ನ
    ಪರ್ರಪಂಚವನರ್ನಯ ಬಣರ್ಣಿಸಯವರೆ
ಧರ್ಯರಾಲರಿಯರಾ, ಹರ್ಕೈಬರಿಸರ್ಕಸರ್ ಮತರ್ತಯ
    ಕರರ್ಯೈಸರಾಂಥರೆಮರ್ಗಳರಿಂದ
ನನಗರೆ ಮರರೆಸರಿಬರಿಡರಿ ಎಲರೆಗಳಯ ಏಕರೆ ನರೆಲಕರ್ಕರೆ
    ಬರೀಳಯಂತರ್ತವರೆ ಎಂದಯ

ಪರ್ರರೀತರಿ ನಮರ್ಮರೊಂದರಿಗರೆ ಒಂದರೆರಡಯ

ಖುತುಗಳ ಕರಾಲ ಮರಾತರ್ರ ಉಳರಿಯುತರ್ತದರೆ
    ಎಂದು
ಅವನ ಚಳರಿಗರಾಲದ ಕಣರ್ಣುಗಳು, ಅವನ ಬರೇಸರಿಗರೆ
    ಮುಂಗರ್ಗುಳರ್ನಗರೆಯನರ್ನು ಮರರೆಸರಿಬರಿಡರಿ
ನನಗರೆ ಪರಿಸು ಮರಾತರಿನಲರ್ಲರಿ ಬರೀಳರ್ಕರೊಟರ್ಟ
    ಅವನ ತುಂಟರಿಗಳನು ಮರರೆಸರಿಬರಿಡರಿ.

AUTUMN
Reshma Ramesh, India

Autumn are you as pretty as the saffron flowers in
    Pampore

Or as yellow as the shedding Chinar leaves in Kash-
    mir?

Are you riding your bicycle under a canopy of Crim-
    son

Or rowing a boat in the blue waters of the Dal?

Are you talking to the mountains in Dharmashala

Calling Buddha from the yellow trees in Ladhakh

Writing poems on fading Maple leaves?

Are you watching the shadow less October Skies

Or recovering from the dizziness of the falling leaves?

Autumn do what you do so well, colour my world

With Dhalias, Hibiscus and Chrysanthemums to

Make me forget that leaves fall for a reason and

Love stays with you only for a couple of seasons

Make me forget that his wintery eyes, his summer
    smiles

Make me forget his lips that whispered good byes.

OCTOBRIANA
Stephanos Stephanides, Cyprus

I will sing to you before the night is over
Month of dust and dirty sweetness
Mother of the rosary and red square
Time for Papa Benedictus to chant
Rosarium virginis Mariae
Apologetica for the infidels
And for Octobriana fucking Vladimir
in Lenin square
people's popular party
turning into progressive political pornography

And I recall that Indian summer when
Gurgench pissed in every river
From Rome to Rimini
Leaving graffiti under every bridge
Tras Tyberis
Erranti eretici erotici he hummed
A feast for Fellini's eye

My October
Tyrants Iulius and Augustus
Have turned you to the tenth month
And now like you I find
My days of the dog-star left behind

So this year let us make a truce
Month and mother of calendula and tourmaline
My brain has lost its sequence
Scorpius still chases my tail
And I still ferry the stars into the sky
Do save my vitality for another Indian summer

Lamenting a lack but daring to hope
Between a mountain too stolid
And a sea too restless
Days are too brief
We all shall be
What this is now
Time is only in the heart
In this my time of vintage

So let me tell you
Iulius
Augustus
Vladimirus
Benedictus
The world is still crazy
And there is more to Octobriana
Than I can still O
Or ever imagine

ΕΞΟΔΟΣ
Β
Σουλεϊμάν Αλάγιαλη-Τσιαλίκ, Ελλάδα

Αστραπιαία περνάνε οι μέρες
οι ώρες, οι στιγμές ...
Κι όταν μέσα από ένα δωμάτιο κλειστό
του μέσα βγαίνω ανακτόρου,
απορώ στο σκοτάδι πως βρέθηκα λοιπόν
το κοινόβιο σε μιαν άλλη ζωή
(κι έξω απ' τη δική μας ερμηνεία της απάθειας ο
    φωταγωγός)
όπου ποιά δύναμη μαζί σου με φυγάδευσε του
    φθινοπώρου.
Και βγαίνοντας κατανοώ πως ακούγονται
νερά που δεν είναι ...
Ω περιπέτειες της αδημονίας μου
που αναζητούν μεσότιτλο στον Άδη
και στροβιλίζονται μόλις νυχτώσει
στο ετερόκλιτο πάθος του πολιτισμού
με ρυθμούς φρενήρεις
ας εξαντλήσουμε λέω τ' όνειρο
που ενσαρκώνει την επίγεια «ευχαρίστηση
    επικοινωνίας»
υιοθετώντας το χιλιοειπωμένο απόφθεγμα του Ch.
    Baudelaire:
«για να μην είστε οι βασανισμένοι σκλάβοι του
    χρόνου
μεθύστε αδιάκοπα! Με κρασί, με ποίηση ή μ' αρετή».
Και βγαίνοντας κατανοώ πως ακούγονται
νερά που δεν είναι ...
Κι όταν το μάγουλο ακουμπώ
στης κολώνας το αισθησιακό αλάβαστρο

που αίφνης ως άλλο απλώνεται μπροστά μας βάζο
να δεχτεί τα ενύπνια λουλούδια
της χαμένης ευγένειας που πονούσες,
ποιά λόγια απ' το περιστύλιο και ποιός θυμός
με κάνουν να ελπίζω να υπάρχω;

EXODUS
B
Suleiman Alayali-Tsialik, Greece
Translated by A. M. Kasdagli, Greece

How they flash by
those days, those hours and moments...
And when I emerge from a closed room
of the inner palace,
I wonder how I got into the communal darkness
in another life
(and the skylight beyond our own interpretation of
   apathy)
where some autumnal power let me escape with you.
And emerging I realise how they sound
those waters that are not ...
Ah, adventures of my impatience
that seek a subheading in Hades
and swirl at nightfall
in the varied passion of civilization;
at a hectic pace,
I say, let us exhaust the dream
that recasts the earthly pleasure of communication
adopting the familiar words of Baudelaire:
in order to escape the tormented slavery time imposes
be forever drunk! With wine, with poetry or with
   virtue.
And emerging I realise how they sound
those waters that are not ...

And when I rest my cheek
on the sensuous alabaster of the column
that suddenly appears before us like another vase
set to receive the dream flowers
of the lost gentleness whose pain you bore,
what words from the peristyle and what anger
make me hope and exist?

BLICKE
Utz Rachowski, Deutschland

Für Andrzej Wieckowski
und Wlodek Nechamkis

An einem eiskalten Sonntag
im November
und es war nicht „Totensonntag"
verließ mich meine Frau.
Ich spürte im Nacken
die höhnischen Blicke der Nachbarn
als ich nachmittags aus dem Haus ging.
An diesem Tag war ich auf nichts vorbereitet
aber plötzlich zwischen zwei U-Bahn-Stationen
sah ich die gläsernen Augen der Emigration.
Es waren der trunkene Atem ewiger Fremde
die kalte Hand einer Verworfenen die
wiederzutreffen man nicht mehr gerechnet hatte.

Sie lugten vor hinter den aufgeregten
Schlagzeilen der Tagespresse mit denen
die Fahrgäste ihre Gesichter bedeckten
sie saßen auf dem goldenen Rand der Brille
eines Studenten der ethnologischen Wissenschaften
erwarteten mich unter dem tanzenden Herbstlaub
zielloser Rolltreppen
sie sahen mich ohne Gnade.

Es waren die Augen einer Schlange
vor Urzeiten
hatten sie mich aus dem Paradies vertrieben
jetzt zwischen zwei U-Bahn-Stationen
erkannten sie mich wieder.

Während die Gedanken in den Schoß
meiner Frau stachen
tappten sie her vor der einbrechenden
Dunkelheit folgten den Schreien
der Hinterhöfe die wie jeden Tag
qualvoll mit der Dämmerung rangen
aber heute nicht müde wurden
denn es war Sonntag ein eiskalter Nachmittag
im November als ich
in die Augen der Fremde sah.

GLANCES

Utz Rachowski, Germany
translated by Louise E. Stoehr, U.S.A.

for Andrzej Wieckowski
and Wlodek Nechamkis

On an ice-cold Sunday
in November
and it was not Eternity Sunday
my wife left me.
Behind my back I sensed
the mocking glances of my neighbors
in the afternoon as I left the house.
On that day I was not prepared for anything
but suddenly between two subway stations
I saw the glassy eyes of emigration.
It was the drunken breath of the eternal foreign
the cold hand of a castaway whom
no one had counted on meeting again.

They peered out from behind the frantic
headlines of the daily papers with which
the subway riders covered their faces
they rested on the golden rim of the glasses
that were worn by a student of ethnology
waited for me beneath the dancing autumn leaves
of aimless escalators
they watched me without mercy.

It was the eyes of a serpent
aeons ago
they had banished me from Paradise
now between two subway stations
they recognized me again.

While my thoughts stabbed
into my wife's womb
they stumbled ahead of the impending
darkness followed the screams
of the back courtyards that wrestled
torturously with dusk as they do every day
but today they did not grow tired
for it was Sunday an ice-cold afternoon
in November when I
looked into the eyes of the foreign.

HERBSTNACHMITTAG /
ÖSTLICH VON ROM

Uwe Friesel, Deutschland

Für Birgitta

Das Jahr ist spät. Die Farben
Verbrennen rot und gelb, doch
Wie in toter Glut, wie von
Blättern, die fallen.

Winzig kleine Vögel flattern.
Ein Himmelsblau aus Stahl
Entsteigt der Silhouette
Der Berge rings und fern des Meeres.

Dann, unerwartet
Bist du da, ist dein Gesicht,
Ist Deine Haut, Dein Körper
Im Blau des Himmels und der Ferne,

Dein Name im Flügelschlag
Des Vogelschwarms, der südwärts wandert,
Und im Olivenbaum, im Schatten
Des Kalksteinhauses am Weg:

Bist du da.

AUTUMN AFTERNOON /
EAST OF ROME
Uwe Friesel, Germany

For Birgitta

The year is late. The colours
Burn red and yellow, but
As in dead glow, as
By wine leaves falling.

Tiny little birds flutter.
An azure of steel
Rises from the silhouette
Of hilltops near and distant sea.

Then, unexpectedly,
You are there: your face
Your skin, your body
In the sky's blue and afar,

Your name in the flap
Of south-bound birds,
In olive-trees and in the shade
Of a limestone house nearby:

You are there.

EYLÜLDE PARK OTEL
W. B. Bayril, Türkiye

Eylül tüylerini serpti şehre. Altın
tüy sağnağı... Korunamaz ki bundan
hiç kimse? Kasvetli pervaz, ölü
yaz ışıklarıyla yıkanıyor. Eriyor lehim,
yorgun cam ateşiyle meyus
İkindinin. Hatırlamak – hah – nafile!

Zalim koleksiyonu zamanın. Bir otel
de teyellenebilir oraya, kuruttuğu
böcekler gibi keskin eczanın. Tene
sürttükçe derine işleyen ayna tozları,
mürekkeple sevişen melekler, ah –

Dağıldılar fecirle. Saatler iri gül
yapraklarını soyundu. Ne yapsak işte;
akıyor ağır madde, kanlı bir iğne ucunda
çırpınıp duran ömrümüze...

PARK HOTEL IN SEPTEMBER
W. B. Bayril, Turkey
Translated by Hilal Karahan, Turkey

September scattered its feathers over the city.
Feather shower of gold… Impossible
To avoid? Dismal sill,
is washed by dead summer lights.
Solder is melting,
by tired glazing fire of sad
Afternoon. Recalling – ah – futile!

Cruel collection of time. A hotel
also can be tacked there, like
insects that pungent medicine weazened.
Mirror dusts penetrating deeper
rubbing at the skin, angels
making love with ink, ah –

All dispersed at dawn. Hours
undressed their ample rose leaves. Whatsoever we
    may do;
the heavy substance is flowing into our lives
struggling constantly on bloody pinpoints

ΕΞΟΡΙΑ ΤΗΣ ΞΗΡΑΣ

Γιώργος Χουλιάρας, Ελλάδα

Με βασανίζουνε προθέσεις και υποθέσεις
Στη γλώσσα βάζω αρώματα, τα ρήματα
μοσχοβολούν
Τα μάτια βάφω άδικα με τις μπογιές
Κανείς τους δεν με βλέπει πια
Στο σπίτι μένω έγκλειστη, δεν βγαίνω
Δεν έχει θάλασσα εδώ να δω, στον ξένο τόπο

Σε πλοίο σώθηκα όταν ταξίδευα κυνηγημένη
Μέσα στους ναύτες, τη ναυτία, τα ναυτικά
Όπου σταμάτησα υπήρχαν Έλληνες
Δικοί μας άνθρωποι που αγαπούνε το νερό
Δεν τους ζαλίζει όμως η στεριά
Εύκολα παίρνουνε το χρήμα στον λαιμό τους

Μακριά από τη θάλασσα τώρα χάνομαι
Σε κύματα φωνής
Στα δάκρυα χώνομαι φωνάζοντας, θυμάμαι

Πριν φύγεις, σε παρακαλώ, τράβηξε το σεντόνι
Κλείσε την πόρτα ήσυχα, μη με ξυπνάς
Ούτε να με θυμάσαι

Δεν ξέρω άλλο τι να πω, αν πνίγομαι
Γιατί εδώ δεν έχει θάλασσα
Αλλά και η θάλασσα δεν έχει εδώ

EXILE ON LAND

[excerpts from her monologue]
Yiorgos Chouliaras, Greece
Translated by David Mason, U.S.A. & the author

Propositions and suppositions torment me
I put fragrances on my tongue, the verbs smell
sweet
In vain I color my eyes with paints
Nobody sees me any more
I stay shut in the house, I don't go out
There's no sea to look at here, a foreign place

I was saved by ship when I traveled hunted
Among sailors, seasickness, seagoing lore
Wherever I stopped there were Greeks
Our own people, who love the water
But land does not dazzle them
They easily stick their necks into money

Now far from the sea I lose myself
In waves of voices
I dive shouting into tears, I remember

Before you go, please, draw up the bedsheet
Close the door quietly, don't wake me
Nor should you remember me

I don't know what else to say, whether I'm drown-
ing
Because here there is no sea
But also in the sea there is no here

POSTMODERNE ELEGIE
Zorin Diaconescu, Rumänien

inzwischen
kam uns der herbst abhanden
es kümmert sich niemand darum
schließlich reisen wir zwischen jahreszeiten
von heute auf morgen, manchmal
geht es sogar schneller
selbst der wetterfrosch hat das begriffen
und nimmt sich nicht mehr ernst
voraussage der wetters ist
eine kurzweil im oldtimer look
blitze gelten vielleicht als filmeffekte
wolken erzeugt jede gratis software
inzwischen
haben wir andere sorgen
in der schule malt man keine gelb-braune blätter
  mehr
und niemand sammelt noch kastanien
inzwischen
kamen uns mehrere sachen abhanden
niemand will sich darauf einlassen
denn wir können uns solche emotionen
nicht mehr leisten, nicht einmal
inzwischen

POSTMODERN ELEGY

Zorin Diaconescu, Romania

meanwhile
we lost the autumn
nobody cares about it
after all,
we travel between seasons
from one day to the next, sometimes
it works even faster,
the weatherman has realized
what's going on
and does not take himself seriously anymore
he predict the weather
as a distraction in old timer look
flashes may be considered film effects
clouds can be generated with every free software
meanwhile
we have other things to worry about
at school no one paints yellow-brown leaves
  anymore
and nobody is still collecting chestnuts
meanwhile
we have lost several things
and nobody wants to get involved
because of the peril in emotions
we can not afford anymore, not even
meanwhile

BIOGRAPHIES

Ahmet Özer is a Turkish poet, writer, critic, academician. He is writing since 1966. He worked as a Turkish literature teacher in various government schools of Turkey. After retirement, he worked as an academician in Bilkent University Literary Faculty for long years. He has published more than 50 books of poetry, prose and critic. He received many poetry awards and participated in a lot of international festivals.

Alexandru Cetăţeanu is a Canadian citizen of a Romanian origin and a famous international poet and journalist. In 2001 he founded the ACSR (The Canadian Romanian Writers' Association) and in 2007 the "Destine Literare", an international cultural and literary review. He has participated in many international poetry festivals. His poems have been translated into English, French, Hindu, Chinese, Japanese, and many other foreign languages.
Translator: **Muguraş Maria Vnuck** is an award winning Romanian/American poet and translator of literature into English, French and Romanian, with books published and launched in the United States of America, India, France, Canada, Romania, Turkey.

Ali Al Hazmi from Saudi Arabia is an international awarded poet who participated in numerous recitals of poetry inside and outside of Saudi Arabia: International Poetry Festival Costa Rica 2013- Toledo,

Spain 2014 - Punta del Este, Uruguay 2015- Madrid. Spain 2016- Havana, Cuba 2016- Medellín, Colombia 2016-Istanbul-Turkey, 2016- Roma 2017-Romania 2017

Ali Günvar is a Turkish poet and writer. He graduated from Saint Joseph High School, Robert College and İTÜ Architecture Faculty. He was one of editors of *Üç Çiçek* and *Şiir Atı* poetry magazines. He has 5 poetry and 1 assay books. He has many poetry awards and his poems are translated to many languages. He is in jury of Seyhan Erözçelik and Ahmet Hamdi Tanpınar

Anna Nasiłowska is a Polish poet, writer, recognized specialist in literature for the Institute of Literary Research in Warsaw and since 2017 the President of the Association of Polish Writers. Her career started very early, first poems were published in 1977. Now she participates in editions of dictionary and encyclopedically works. Author of *History of Polish Literature* three biographies, novels, short stories, essays and various critical revues. Her publications saw the light in Russian, Bulgarian, Hebrew, German and English. Latest volume of poems was inspired by many travels across Greece.

Anna Würth is an author and photographic artist. She worked for 30 years as a journalist in Hamburg. Her poems and short stories have been published in 80 anthologies and in her book *Aphrodite.Lovestoned* by Wachholtz. She received the Literary Sponsorship Award of GEDOK. Public readings in several countries. In her *Literary Pictures* she combines her work with her photography, which were exhibited in Germany, Denmark and Cyprus.

Translator: **Anna Engeln** is a German poet, writer, child-therapist and social researcher for socio-cultural changes in Europe. **Todd Brown** from U.S.A. lives in England, is a jazz musician, entrepreneur and business consultant.

Aristea Papalexandrou has published five books of poetry: *Dio onira prin* (*Two Dreams Ago*, 2000), *Allote allou* (*Once, Elsewhere*, 2004), *Odika ptina* (*Songbirds*, 2008), *Ypogeios* (*Underground*, 2012), *Mas propserna* (*It's Passing Us By*, 2015). She has studied music and Medieval and Modern Greek Literature. She works as an editor. For her last book, *It's Passing Us By*, she had honored by the Academy of Athens, in December 2017.

Translator: **Yannis Goumas** is a poet, novelist, actor, translator and composer. His work includes collections of poems in English and Greek.

Barbara Pogačnik, poet, translator and literary critic has published four poetry books: Poplave (Inundations, 2007), V množici izgubljeni papir (Sheets of Paper Lost in the Crowd, 2008), Modrina hiše / The Blue of the House (2013) and Alica v deželi plaščev (Alice in the Land of Coats, 2016). Her poetry in translations has partially appeared in 30 languages. She has participated in more than 50 different literary manifestations all over the world. More than 150 authors have appeared in her own translations.

Translator: **Ana Jelnikar** is one of the foremost translators of contemporary Slovenian poetry into English and a researcher.

Barry Stevenson, Poet and translator. He wrote his first poem at 13, his second at 15 and then, from 17 on, he doesn't know how many. When he was 47, a rarely-heard, fearless inner voice told him that, good or bad, he was, always had been and always would be a *poet* and whether he liked it or not or ever composed another line was irrelevant – *"it's what you* are, *so just get on with it"*. All this in a split second. So he did. The result was *The Western Park* (2,500 ll.) and *Tigertale* (still in the making) with, in all, some 200-odd satellites in tow.

Betül Tarıman is a Turkısh poet. She studied History at Hacettepe University. Her first poem appeared in Kıyı magazine in 1992. Other magazines that have included her work are Varlık, Gösteri, Sözcükler, E Edebiyet, Damar, Yasakmeyve, Adam Sanat and Edebiyet ve Eleştiri. She was the recipient of the Necatigil Poetry Prize in 2005. She currently writes literary ads and essays for Cumhuriyet Kitap.

Burkhard P. Bierschenck spent a part of his youth in the Middle and the Far East. He studied journalism, history and literature. He speaks and writes in German, English and French. Apart from his career as Journalist, reaching top positions of Editorial Director and General Manager, he wrote more than 25 books, mostly novels and poetry. His acclaimed poetry became part of school curriculum.

Chloe Koutsoubelli's literary journey lasts thirty five years. Her first collection of poems was published in 1984, when she was twenty two years old. Ever since, she has published eight collections of poems, two novels and two theatrical plays. Poems and short stories of hers were published in most of the literary magazines of her country. Many of her poems were translated in English, German, Italian, Spanish and Bulgarian. She has participated in Greek and foreign anthologies of poems.

Translator: **Anna Koustinoudi** has taught a number of literary and academic writing courses as an adjunct lecturer at the Department of English Literature (School of English).

Christine Geweke is a painter, sculptures and lyricist. She is a member of the Hamburger Autorenvereinigung (Hamburg Writers Association). On 8.3.2009 she launched the "Charta der SchriftstellerInnen für die Wahrung des Weltfriedens" ('Charta of authors for preserving world peace') and has started publishing anthologies with peace as the theme. She has published five volumes of poetry.

Cigdem Hicran Yorgancioglu from Istanbul is a cross-discipline globe-trotter (106 Countries completed as of May 2018), a Turkish economist, instructor, auditor, mentor, judicial expert at Criminal and Civil Courts, academician (University), Visiting Professor (seminar basis), columnist, artist (Poet, creative writer, painter) and Diplomatic journalist.

Claudia Piccinno is a teacher and a scholastic referent land for education at reading. Operating in more than seventy anthologies, she has been member of the jury in many national and international literary prizes. She was an italian editor for the international literary magazine Rosetta World Literatura in Turkey and for Atunis Magazine in Albania. She gained almost 150 awards in poetry competitions

Deborah D'Agostino is a poetess, writer, cultural Promoter. Lives in Rome, Italy, where for the past twenty years has been an organizer and presenter of cultural events. Winner of numerous national and international prizes for her poetry published in anthologies, magazines and art catalogues. Presents creative writing laboratories in the Italian schools and Literary meetings, has been Jury of Literary Prizes.

Dorel Cosma, Romania, holds a B.A. in Journalism, radio-tv producer, senior editor of several newspapers and magazines, chairman of the I.G.F. World Folklore Union, manager of the Palace of Culture, the most important cultural institution of his hometown. Author of several books published in Romania, Bulgaria, Italy, Greece, Egypt, France, Argentina, Germany, Austria, Spain and the U.S.A.

Emel Koşar is currently a faculty member at Turkish Language and Literature Department of Faculty of the Arts and Sciences of Mimar Sinan University of Fine Arts. She has published her poetry and essays on Turkish literature in various literary magazines. She published her research and review books, scientific and literary works she edited, and 5 poetry collections.

Translator: **Yaprak Damla Yıldırım** graduated from Boğaziçi University Management and Western Languages and Literatures departments.

Emina Kamber is a poetess, painter and a teacher of exile literature and art, born in Kakanj, Bosnia-Herzegovina and living in Hamburg, Germany since 1968. She is deputy chairwoman of the German Writers Union (VS) in Hamburg, a member of the German Exile PEN. In 1988 she established the international Literature Club „La Bohemina".

Emina Kamber has published books in different languages and received various Literature Awards.

Ertuğrul Özüaydın is a Turkish poet, writer and critic. He published his first poems in Eskişehir Sakarya Newspaper (1981). His poems are translated into many languages and he was invited to many national and international poetry festivals. He is editor of Patika Poetry Magazine since 2002 and Contemporary Turkish Language Magazine since 2016. He is the asistant president of Turkish Language Association

Fethi Sassi is a tunusian poet, writer and translator. His work includes prose, poetry, short poems and haiku. He has been translated every of his poems into English.

Gino Leineweber has been active as a poet since 1998. From 2003 to 2008 he was editor / editor in chief of the Buddhist Monthly Magazine (Buddhistische Monatsblätter). He has three poetry books published so far and poems in international anthologies and magazines. He has received several awards. He has participated in many international poetry festivals. His poems have been translated into about ten languages. Since 2013 he has been President of the Three Seas Writers' and Translators' Council (TSWTC) based in Rhodes, Greece.

Gonca Özmen studied English language and Literature at the Istanbul University. She took her M. A. degree in 2008 and finished her Ph.D. in 2016. Her first poem was published in 1997 when she was 15. She was one of the editors of literary translation magazine called Ç.N. (Çevirmenin Notu) and PulBiber. She is one of the editors of the magazine Çevrimdışı Istanbul. On the advisory board of Bursa Nilüfer International Poetry Festival and the magazine, Turkish Poetry Today. Member in the Three Seas Writers' and Translators' Council (TSWTC) based in Rhodes, Greece. Her poems are translated into Spanish, French, English, German, Slovenian, Persian, Czech Language, Polish, Ukrainian and Slovak.

Translator: **George Messo** is an English poet and translator. He was the editor of Near East Review from 2001 to 2007. Messo is a Fellow of the Royal Asiatic Society. He is the editor of the Turkish Modern Poets Series for Red Hand

Books, and the editor of the bi-lingual journal Turkish Poetry Today.

Gurinder Singh Kalsi is a poet and storywriter. He has 17 books to his credit. He is a National Award winning writer. His writings are about life and nature. He also writes for children. By profession he is a science teacher in a government school. He is also a good painter.

Hilal Karahan is a Turkish poetess, writer, translator and medical doctor. She has been writing since 2000. She has six poem, three prose books and many selected poem books published in different languages. She has joined to many international collective books, bilingual poetry almanacs. Since she is intercontinental director of World Festival of Poetry (WFP) organisation, she is in organisation committee of many international poetry festivals. She is a member of Turkish PEN, Turkish Authors Association and Turkish Language Society. Since 2017, she is a member of publishing council of international bilingual poetry magazines of *Absent, Rosetta Word Literature* and *Sahitya Anand*.

Holly Iglesias' books include three collections of poetry— *Sleeping Things* (Press 53), *Angles of Approach* (White Pine Press) and *Souvenirs of a Shrunken World* (Kore Press)—and a work of criticism, *Boxing Inside the Box: Women's Prose Poetry* (Quale Press). She has received fellowships from the National Endowment for the Arts, the North

Carolina Arts Council, the Edward Albee Foundation, and the Massachusetts Cultural Council.

Jenny Lkhagvasuren started writing poems in 2013 and her first book of poetry *The Happy Lady* has been published both in Mongolian and English. Her translation of poems from Mongolian to English mostly have been also been published in poetry books. Some of her poems have been published in Illinois State in U.S.A., Turkey, Italy and Albany. She also works on translations of novels and poetry books Mongolian-English-Mongolian.

Juan C. Tajes, Montevideo, Co-founder of Grupo Vanguardia in 1963. Edited poetry work:
Canto al Hombre 1963; *Cristos de arcilla* 1964/1965; *Tantango* 1996; *Time of words* 2016; And in many poetry anthologies all over the world.

Julio Pavanetti is the President of the Int'l Poets Association 'Liceo Poético de Benidorm'. Director of the Int'l Poetry Festival "FIPBECO", Spain. Director of the Poetry Collection "Azul" of Enkuadres Publishers. Spain. Member of the "Association of Spanish Writers and Artists", the "Spanish Collegiate Association of Writers" and the "World Poetry Movement". He has published 13 books and has been included in more than 50 international anthologies. He has received several awards. He has participated in many international poetry festivals. His poems have been translated into 15 languages.

Liana Sakelliou is a poet, translator, critic, and editor. She is the author of eighteen books, most recently: *Where the Wind Blows Softly* (poetry collection, Typothito, 2017), *Creative Reading, Writing, and Living: volume 1, The Novel* (co-authored with W. Schultz, Gutenberg, 2013), *Prends-moi comme une photo* (poetry collection, L' Harmattan, 2012), and *Portrait before Dark* (poetry collection, Typothito, 2010). She wrote a monograph as well as edited and co-authored the translation of 60 Poems –165 Letters–Notes by Emily Dickinson (*Emily Dickinson: Because I could not bear to live aloud,* Gutenberg, 2012), a monograph on *H.D.'s Trilogy: Co-authored Translation–Notes* (Gutenberg, 1999), as well as a monograph on *Gary Snyder: The Poetics and Politics of Place* (Odysseas, 1998). Among her awards are two Fulbright Fellowships in the US, several fellowships from the British Council, the Marie Curie Intra-European Fellowship, the Stanley J. Seeger Visiting Research Fellowship at Princeton University, and residencies at West Dean College— University of Sussex, and at the Casa d' Escrita-Universidade de Coimbra—Portugal. Her poems have been widely anthologized and translated into several languages.

Lily Exarchopoulou is a writer. She has published three novels, one book of poetry and a Greek reader. Her latest novel was I on the short list of the Athens Prize for Literature. Her short stories have been published in anthologies, newspapers and literary magazines and one of her novels was the gist of the eponymous play staged in a prominent Athenian theater. She has translated from English into Greek works by world - acclaimed writers such as D.H. Lawrence, L. Durrell, E.Said, J.Berger et. al. She is a literary reviewer, columnist and has taught Greek and English Language and Literature as well as Ancient History in high schools and History of European Literature in the Greek Open University.

Maren Schönfeld, poetess and journalist. She has three poetry books published so far. In 2017 she received the Poetry Award from the Hamburg Writers' Association (Writers' Association Hamburg).

Marian Eikelhof is a poet who works in her daily life as a psychologist leading her own consultancy firm, named Psychologisch Adviesbureau Ariadne. Her work inspires her to write about the emotional aspects of existence. Not only she describes feelings of love, intimacy and desire, but also she reflects in her poetry on sad, fragile experiences and she criticizes dehumanisation. Marian has recently published the second edition of her collection of Dutch poems titled *een nulurencontract met het leven* and a first edition of her English collection of poetry carrying the title *a zero-hour contract with life*. Marian is active furthermore active in defending human rights with a special emphasis on the empowerment of women internationally. To focus on the peace process with other poets she is continental director of Europe in the World Festival of Poetry and she has just started a foundation together with the Cuban writer Victor Hugo Perez Gallo, under the name "Foundation Literary International".

Marina Savova is an international performing concert pianist. She is Member of Writers Association of Hamburg. Since over 15 years she works together with Gino Leineweber and other authors for music-poetic-interconnected concerts and events. Her musical and poetic performances are an expression of the unit of soul, world and universe.

Mawar Marzuki, a lecturer in English Language at one of the leading Teacher Training College in Malaysia is a bilingual writer, poet, critic, editor and translator. Her poetry anthology *Ajarkan Kami Berpuisi* consists English and Malay language poetry. Being Vice President for three established literary forums – Penang Artists Society, Penang Poet Society and Penang Malay's History and Culture Society, she has also travelled across the globe as a writer and poet for several literary festivals across Asia and other continents like Romania, Turkey, and Mongolia.

Mesut Şenol graduated from the Political Science Faculty of Ankara University. Earned his Master's Degree in Public Administration and Public Relations. His five poetry collections were published, and many of his poetry and literary translations appeared in many national and foreign literary publications and anthologies. Attended a number of national and international poetry and literary festivals in the country and abroad, and acting as an organizer for some of them. Received numerous literary awards in the country and abroad. A member of many literary organizations. In May 2016, he was elected to serve for three years on the Executive Board of the Three Seas Writers and Translators Council. He is the Turkey Culture Delegate of the *Liceo Poetico De Benidorm*

Milica Jeftimijević Lilić graduated at the Faculty of Philosophy in Priština, and won a master's degree in philological sciences at the University of Belgrade. She was a professor at the University of Priština, and editor on Belgrade TV. She has published collections of poems, stories and essays.
She received many literary awards and her work is translated into more than 28 languages. She used to be the Vice President of the Association of Writers' of Serbia

Okan Yılmaz graduated from Turkish Language and Literature at Mimar Sinan University of Fine Arts. He currently studies for master degree of New Turkish Literature at Yıldız Technical University. His poems, essays and interviews are being published in various prestigious literary magazines such as *Varlık, Kitap-lık, Mühür*, and *Yasakmeyve*.
Translator: Yasemin Üşümüş graduated from Mimar Sinan University of Fine Arts with a degree. In 2018, she won her masters degree about "New Turkish Language".

Osman Öztürk served for long years at various departments of the Directorate General of the Security of the Turkish Interior Ministry holding high level positions. He also worked at the Turkish embassies in Washington D.C. and Paris. In 2007 he published his poetry collection called *The Bucket*, and it was followed respectively by the publications of *The Season Of Cherry Laurel, The Missing Page, The Autumn Loneliness* and *You Were Much Of The Green As Well As The Blue*. In his books, he expresses his feelings ranging from love to loneliness, from joy to sorrow and the different circumstances of a human being.

Raed Anis Al-Jishi is a poet and translator from Qateef/Saudi Arabia. He has published one novel, nine volumes of poems in Arabic and one, *Bleeding Gull: Look, Feel, Fly*, in English wich was translated into Italian and Siberian language as well. Alongside a career as a writer, he teaches high school chemistry. He is a feminist and human rights activist, and works on issues involving children and literacy.
Translator: **Amira Rammah** received a BA in English Language and Literature, and pursued an MA in Cross Cultural Studies both from *Institut Supérieur des Langues de Tunis* (University of Carthage). She translates from Arabic and French

Reshma Ramesh is a bilingual poet writing in English and Kannada. Her poetry book *Reflection of Illusions* (Writers Workshop) has been presented in the International Read and Share Conference attended by Asian Countries in Malaysia in April 2017 and PULARA 8. She is the recipient of Savitribai Phule National Women Achiever Award 2018, a Fellow of the Regal World of Scribes and a member of World Congress of Poets and has presented her poetry in the 2018 UNESCO Istanbul festival, 37th World Congress of poets Mongolia and Pulara 7 International Poetry and Folk Song Festival Malaysia. She has been a speaker in the Bangalore Literature Festival 2017 and Language Festival 2018 and is a prominent voice in one of the most important poetry platforms Kavya Sanje in Bangalore. She practices Dental Surgery in Bangalore.

Stephanos Stephanides is a poet, essayist and memoirist, translator, ethnographer, documentary filmmaker, and retired as Professor of English and Comparative Literature at the University of Cyprus in 2017. His most recent publication *The Wind Under My Lips* is a bilingual anthology (English/Greek). Previous representative publications include *Translating Kali's Feast: the Goddess in Indo-Caribbean Ritual and Fiction* (2000) and *Blue Moon in Rajasthan and other poems* (2005).

Suleiman Alayiali-Tsialik is working as a professional jeweler in the Old Middle Age Town of Rhodes. He is a member to the 'Chamber of Literary and Good Arts of Dodecanese' and Board Member of "The International Center of Writers and Translators of Rhodes". He has published six Collections of Poetry: *Ephemeral Light, Curbs of narcosis, Nocturnal Soundings, Heaven's Clock Has Been Stopped, Water-colour* and *In Beginning of the Coincidences to Flashes*.

Utz Rachowski was a former political prisoner in East Germany and sentenced to 27 months in jail because of five of his poems. He has published 14 books of stories, essays, and poetry. Most recently, he received the 2007 Reiner Kunze-Prize and the 2008 Hermann-Hesse-Stipendium. 2013 he was nominated for Pushcart Prize in the US. 2014; Nikolaus-Lenau-Prize. 2017; and received the Prose-Prize from the *Society for Contemporary American Literature in German*.

Translator: **Louise E. Stoehr** is an Associate Professor of German at Stephen F. Austin State University in Nacogdoches, Texas. She has published numerous literary translations by authors including Günter Grass, Elfriede Jelenik, Hans-Joachim Schädlich, Sarah Kirsch, and Uwe Kolbe.

Uwe Friesel, poet, author, translator (Vladimir Nabokov, John Updike, Ben Jonson). 1991-1994 First President of the united German Writers Association after the fall of the Berlin Wall. Co-founder of the international UNESCO-Lit-Centres in Visby and Rhodes. Rewards: Villa Massimo in Rome, Writer in residence in Hamburg and Berlin. German Literature Fonds. Member of PEN.

W. B. Bayril is a Turkish Poet, Writer and Creative Director. Since 1980, his poems and articles about poetry, literature and painting have been published in many reviews and newspapers. He published four poetry and two prose books and has received literature awards. He has been working in advertising business as creative director in İstanbul for 30 years. He is a member of jury of Seyhan Erözçelik Poetry Award.

Yiorgos Chouliaras is a Greek poet, essayist, prose writer, and translator. In 2014 he was awarded an Academy of Athens prize for his work in its entirety. His poetry in English translation has been published in major periodicals and anthologies, as well as in Bulgaria, Croatia, France, Italy, Japan, Lithuania, and Turkey among other countries. He has worked as a university lecturer, correspondent, press counselor at Greek Embassies, and advisor to cultural institutions.
Translator: **David Mason** is the former Poet Laureate of Colorado. An award-winning poet, essayist, librettist, and translator, his most recent collection of poetry is *The Sound*.

Zorin Diaconescu graduate of the English Language Departement of the Faculty of Letters at Babes-Bolyai University, Cluj, Romania. Building a bridge between Romanian and English – a job for a lifetime. Occasionally he writes poetry. He also published a documentary book about the year 1989. He writes in and translates into/from: Romanian, German and English.

Also released in Verlag Expeditionen

Gino Leineweber (Ed.)
Let's talk about Summer – International Poetry

Softcover, 112 Pages, Published October 2017,
ISBN 978-3-943863-75-1

In an Exhibition in an ArtGarden in Rhodes, Greece, 37 poets from Bosnia and Herzegovina, Cyprus, Georgia, Germany, Greece, India, Italy, the Netherlands, Poland, Rhodes, Romania, Spain, Turkey, the United Kingdom, the United States and Uruguay presented their poems. The presentation was in English as well as in the respective mother tongue. It was a unique occasion to have such an international selection.This book will address all lovers of poetry with the wonderful collection.

Gino Leineweber (Ed.)
Wayfarers – Stories, Essays, Poems

Softcover, 380 Pages, Published May 2017,
ISBN 978-3-943863-66-6

This book is part of the publisher's Literature Caravan Edition. A group of writers and poets traveling together on an expedition to a certain topic.

The Island of Rhodes was the caravanserai of a journey initiated by the Hamburg Writers Association and the Three Seas Writers' and Translators' Council

The literary travel subject was The Strange in Us. The fruits of this journey with its one-week workshop in September 2016 is published in this multilingual book of poems, essays, and stories by twelve writers from six countries.

Gino Leineweber
Hello Darkness – Poems 2010 - 2014

Softcover, 74 Pages, Published April 2017,
ISBN 978-3-943863-19-2

This Poetry Book contains poems in three sections, Hello Darkness, Romance, and Literature.

It is the third poetry book by the German poet Gino Leineweber and the first one in English language.